Praise for

The Inner Advantage

It is easy to dismiss the contemporary mindfulness movement as a popular trend, not something for serious professionals. The strength of Patton Hyman's book, and what differentiates it from the plethora of mindfulness books now on the market, is that it is directed specifically to professionals and the contexts in which they operate. Drawing on his own decades of lawyering and meditating and teaching professionals to meditate, Patton presents both the how and the why of meditation in clear, accessible language that is always oriented to the challenges and opportunities that professionals experience every day.

–DAVID ROME,
Author of *Your Body Knows the Answer: Using Your Felt Sense to Solve Problems, Effect Change, and Liberate Creativity*

Patton's no nonsense approach to meditation is insightful as well as practical. He brings the analytical mind of a lawyer to a topic that at first might seem vague but through anecdotes and clear instructions, introduces the reader to powerful practices that are invaluable for professionals pursuing a life of meaning and purpose.

– SUSAN SKJEI, PH.D, Director,
Authentic Leadership Center at Naropa University

The Inner Advantage is a superb exploration of mindfulness that effectively weaves together mindfulness insights and experiential practices, and does so in manner that is as practical as it is profound. The clarity of Hyman's writing offers readers an opportunity to meaningfully integrate mindfulness into their lives, personally and professionally. This important book comes at the right time and delivers its timeless message with a compassion and wisdom borne out of Hyman's personal experience, a testament to its authenticity and usefulness.

– SCOTT L. ROGERS, M.S., J.D., Director,
Mindfulness in Law Program, University of Miami School of Law, Miami, Florida

The **Inner** Advantage

leadership
work
clarity
presence creativity
adaptability diplomacy
intuition insight livelihood
communication challenge

*Applying Mindfulness In Business
and Law—and Everywhere Else!*

Patton Hyman

Published by AMT Press
Barnet, VT

ISBN: 978-0-692-64517-8

BOOK & COVER DESIGN: Bob Schram, Bookends Design

DEDICATION

To Carol

ACKNOWLEDGEMENTS

Many people have contributed to this book's coming to existence, and those contributions took many forms.

After teaching meditation for many years, I got under way with professional presentations thanks to Jason Newman, my friend and fellow practitioner, who introduced me to Kevin Ryan of the Vermont Bar Association. Kevin was enthusiastic about a mindfulness program, and with the able assistance of Laura Welcome, I had the chance to make many presentations to lawyers, the source of a lot of what I learned and present in this book. That experience was further cultivated at American University, where Ruth Zaplin and Bob Tobias sponsored my mindfulness presentations to the Key Executive Leadership program.

The directors of Applied Mindfulness Training all read drafts of this book and made invaluable suggestions. Specific thanks to Reeve Lindbergh, Bill Brauer, Michael Carroll, Richard Reoch, and Tom Wales.

Others who made a variety of contributions are Rich Fernandez, Len Riskin, Scott Rogers, Marc Lesser, Robert Chender, David Rome, David Tripp, and Susan Skjei, as well as numerous individuals who helped me develop professional programs through Applied Mindfulness Training, or as it was known in the early days, Tail of the Tiger. These include Barbara Heffernan, Madeline Bruser, Doug Lindner, Patricia Anderson, Michael Carroll, Jacqueline Kaufman, David Rome, Vicki Tansey, Jill Satterfield, Susan Piver, and David Sable.

Thanks also to my professional editor Claire Wyckoff. In-house editing credits go to my wife and son, Carol and Andrew, who were ruthlessly (in the best sense) helpful.

Mike Slattery introduced me to Sid Walker, who wrote the Foreword and introduced me to Bob Schram, who designed the book. Hazel Bercholz made invaluable suggestions about design.

My deepest appreciation goes out to my daughter, Sarah, my son, Andrew, my cousin David Tripp, my sister-in-law Beverly Robertson, my brother, Tom, and his wife, Jennie, and the rest of my family for their unconditional support during my near-fatal illness. This book is dedicated to my wife, Carol, without whose efforts over many months I would likely not have survived. She is the love of my life, and I can't imagine it without her.

Finally, I would not know about meditation were it not for Chögyam Trungpa and his son, Sakyong Mipham Rinpoche, to whom I will always be grateful.

The Perfect Man for the Job

— BY SID WALKER

Meditation has played a major role in my life and career. As a sales performance coach for over thirty years, primarily to financial advisors, I'm often asked by my clients about meditation. They want to know what they can read and how to get started. If you type *meditation* into a search engine, you get over one hundred million results, a daunting number. Add the perception that meditation is cloaked in mystery to the fact that its practice comes to us from the eastern part of the world, and finding a simple and comfortable way to begin can be a challenge.

This is the gift of Patton Hyman and his book on meditation-based mindfulness, *The Inner Advantage*. It is the perfect introduction for westerners and especially business and professional people, who tend to be analytical. Patton, a former partner in a leading law firm in Atlanta, has been teaching people how to meditate for over thirty years. His seminars for attorneys have gotten great reviews, with participants enjoying the process as well as being pleased with the subsequent results. And as everybody knows, lawyers are a tough crowd.

Patton's teaching style reflects his personality—simple, genuine, and humorous—as well as conveys insights that are the culmination of thousands of hours of experience. You will appreciate that he invites you to experiment and discover what has meaning for you. That's the best kind of coach. And even though Patton would be a worthy opponent in a legal negotiation, he is also a gentle soul, which comes through in his writing.

Focusing on the present moment through meditation is training that allows us to access a higher intelligence which brings with it practical benefits. *The Inner Advantage* allows you to move toward greater peace and prosperity. Let Patton show you how to take the important first steps into a new and profound understanding of yourself. You will be glad you walked this path with him.

–SIDNEY C. WALKER
Author of *Trust Your Gut*

CONTENTS

Preface

Introduction

PART ONE:
The Added Value of Presence

PART TWO:
Fear: The Untapped Asset

PART THREE:
Everyday Applications

PART FOUR:
The Dividends of Mindfulness

Appendices

When I first suggested developing a mindfulness meditation-based training for lawyers, I got an incredulous response. "What? Lawyers are so analytical. They'll never be interested." To everyone's surprise but mine, lawyers quickly took to meditation. It made sense to them, and I've found that being analytical is not an obstacle, but may even be an inducement. For people in business as well as others for whom analytic skills are an important part of their work, being presented with the evidence of their experience makes it easy to see the value of mindfulness.

I discovered mindfulness early in my legal career. In the 1970s, it was unusual for professionals to practice meditation and I came to it by a circuitous route: I was led to meditation by reading Albert Einstein's book describing the theory of relativity (one written for the layperson, of course), which led me to other books on modern physics. Some of those suggested parallels between the insights of physics and Eastern philosophies, and so I began exploring Hinduism and Buddhism.

One author, a Tibetan lama named Chögyam Trungpa, appealed to my practical side: he wrote that while it's fine to read about the philosophy and theory of these traditions, if you really want to know the experience they're talking about, you have to do meditation. Being a business lawyer, I liked the practical approach of his style of mindfulness practice.

At that time Atlanta, where I lived, there was no place to learn this kind of mindfulness, a problem I wouldn't now have there or in almost any other major city. But the book listed a meditation center in Vermont, so I headed there on a two-week vacation to check it out. Being naturally risk-averse, I had an alternate plan to go backpacking on the Appalachian Trail if the place turned out to be too weird.

Arriving in Vermont, I hitchhiked from Montpelier to Barnet and arrived at the center on a beautiful, crisp fall day. A nice woman gave me meditation instruction, after which I had lunch and eagerly awaited the afternoon practice session. At last I was going to find out what this meditation business was all about. Would I be transported into realms of bliss? Would I suddenly understand the riddles of the universe, the meaning of life? Who knew? I was ready, willing, and curious.

The room was arranged with rows of cushions. A woman timing the sitting struck a bronze gong. As the sound slowly faded away, I sat there, breathing (I'd been told to pay attention to that) and trying to get comfortable on the cushion. I remember thinking "Anything else? Is this all I'm supposed to do? Does this make any sense?"

"Well, yes, at least theoretically," I thought. "If I'm going to learn how mind works, observing it makes sense." But I was getting really uncomfortable. Although my instructor had said they'd ring the gong periodically to signal walking meditation, it seemed I'd been sitting for a long time. My thoughts wandered all over the place, from wondering when we'd get up and walk to thinking about how I could ever explain to my co-workers, family, and others back home why I'd traveled 1,200 miles to sit around doing nothing.

I had plenty of time to contemplate this because, as it turned out, the gong didn't ring again for two and a half hours! I had no idea I had let myself in for such rigorous discipline, much less that it would feel like torture. Partly that was because of the physical discomfort of staying still so long, cross-legged, on a cushion. But even more uncomfortable was my nonstop mental chatter. I'd never noticed before how relentlessly my mind churned out thoughts. (By the way, I was never subjected to such a long, uninterrupted period of sitting again. Thank goodness!)

Glimpsing that tenacious mental momentum made me want to see more. After all, everything I experienced was filtered through my mind, and meditation was supposed to be a tool for polishing the lens. I would discover it to be an effective one, but because of the prevailing attitude that it was something odd, I mostly kept quiet about my meditation practice while engaged in practice with my fellow lawyers.

Eventually I decided to "come out" about my unusual avocation when the opportunity to attend a three month meditation program arose and I really wanted to do it. Because the firm had no standing policy about taking time off beyond the normal vacation allowance, the resulting firm politics meant negotiations about appropriate compensation adjustments and a year's delay before eventually my absence was approved. However, it would turn out that doubt had been raised about my "commitment to law practice" which affected my share in the firm's subsequent annual distributions.

The irony of that is now clear: I knew that mindfulness could only enhance my performance as a lawyer; indeed mindfulness has come to be taught in bar association-approved trainings nation-wide. It's especially gratifying to see that now, decades later, the word about mindfulness is getting out to people through mainstream media outlets such as the *Wall Street Journal*, the *Harvard Business Review*, and others.

Not only does mindfulness help those who practice it become more effective in their work, it also lightens up the process of working, even when we're working very hard. For this reason, I long wanted to find a way to make mindfulness available in professional contexts. Eventually that wish would come true.

Over the last decade I've had the privilege of training people who work in business, law, healthcare, government, and the arts in meditation-based mindfulness. My hope is that this book will make mindfulness and meditation accessible to an even wider range of people, who can then share the "real life" benefits with others. Because the way we work affects those around us, among the real benefits of mindfulness are what might be termed attitude enhancements.

For example, one of my extra-curricular activities during my legal career in Atlanta was serving on a bar association committee charged with drafting Georgia's "second generation" condominium act. The original act, having been crafted on the assumption that condominiums were always housed in high-rise buildings, was not flexible; as condominium development took off, a more workable scheme was desirable. Attorneys from a number of large Atlanta firms also served on the committee; my task was to be the principal draftsman. Lawyers regularly deal in great detail and tedium and this project brought both in spades. But instead of getting bogged down, I found mindfulness helping me stay fresh and cheerful, something for which others on the project expressed their appreciation. One advantage of applying mindfulness is that it allows one to relax in the midst of activity without losing the edge needed to do the work well. In that respect it enhances not only one's skills, but also one's quality of life.

Mindfulness helps people recognize something very real and basic about themselves and about other people, something that's an actual experience and not just wishful thinking. When people access mindful presence, they may well come to believe, as I have, that human beings, for all their foibles, are a tremendous resource. The practices described in this book are designed to help bring about that realization.

How Is This Book Different?

There are many books about mindfulness these days. Two things set this one apart:

1. First, this book's emphasis is on applying mindfulness to whatever a person chooses to do. It discusses activities frequently encountered in business, in law, and in other professional pursuits to which mindfulness lends a helpful perspective and strength.
2. Second, this book tells how to relate with nervousness and other manifestations of fear in a way that helps us become more engaged and present in challenging activities. Fear doesn't have to be an obstacle.

The time spent paying attention to our *inner* experience changes the way we engage the *outer* world. Whatever the nature of our work, the constantly changing environment (economic, political, personal and otherwise) presents unending challenges. We need to be alert and open to meet them.

This is not a scholarly book. It's based on my own experience as a lawyer, practitioner and program leader over several decades, and on the experience of others I've worked with. You won't find a lot of studies and data referenced in this book. That's because its premise is that mindfulness meditation only matters to the extent it makes a difference in life as you live it.

To those who would argue that this approach is anecdotal and not "scientific," I can only plead in its defense that life is anecdotal.

INTRODUCTION

Has this ever happened to you?

You're in a meeting with your boss when you suddenly realize you haven't heard a thing he or she has said for several seconds (or minutes, you're not sure). Not wanting your boss to think you weren't paying attention, you try to figure out—from what he or she is saying now—just what you must have missed.

Or you're in a meeting and someone asks you a question. You were distracted and don't even know what the question was about. To compound the matter, you try to listen to what is being said now *simultaneously* with trying to figure out what was *already* said, which divides your attention further, making it harder to hear and respond to the current discussion.

Being awakened from distraction suddenly in this way can be very uncomfortable. It can even generate a panicky sensation, especially if you want to try to avoid letting people know you weren't listening.

Here's another slightly different example:

You're making a presentation to your boss (or customer, client, or colleague), and you realize you haven't heard a thing *you've* been saying. You don't even remember where you are in your discussion. In addition to the awkwardness that brings, you find yourself wondering whether your presentation has been as boring for your listeners as it has been to you.

Being distracted doesn't necessarily have anything to do with the value of what's being said by others or by ourselves; rather it reflects a more basic situation we suffer from—being so habituated to involvement in our own thoughts that distraction happens automatically and often goes almost unnoticed. The result is loss of focus.

Happily, the situation isn't hopeless; with training in mindfulness, distraction becomes less frequent and we notice it sooner so that we can remain present more of the time.

What's more, reducing distraction is just the beginning. As mindfulness increases, it opens us to a more complete, fulfilling, and enjoyable relationship to our lives, whether at work, at home, or anywhere else. That's the advantage we're talking about in this book, and it goes far beyond improving our presentations or being able to track conversations. All we have to do is learn how to cultivate mindfulness, and then apply it wherever we are.

What Is Applied Mindfulness?

Some people think that "mindfulness" means noticing every particular detail in every situation we encounter. This is a misconception. Mindfulness is actually a state of relaxed awareness (in this book it will be called "presence") in which we approach all situations with an open attitude of alert attention.

Applied mindfulness is based on a simple formula: if we are to be mindful, we have to be present, and if we are going to be present, we have to learn how *not* to be distracted.

Being present without distraction is something we can all do because it's completely natural. The challenge is to learn to cultivate presence intentionally, so that it doesn't just happen erratically. As we cultivate presence, we become capable of inducing mindfulness, learning how to be present in every moment, enhancing our lives at work, at home, and even when we're just hanging out with no particular purpose.

When we train in mindfulness, paying attention is central to what we do; however, before engaging in mindfulness training, the simple act of paying attention isn't something we're especially sensitive to. Sure, we've all been ordered to "Pay attention!" by a teacher, boss, or parent, but those admonitions were directed at the content, not to the attention itself. When we focus solely on content, our minds are busy as an airport. We may never even notice presence, nor give much thought to how this lack of attention affects the way we see the world, or deal with others, or do our jobs. The premise of this book is that cultivating presence and applying mindfulness can correct that state of affairs.

But how do we apply mindfulness? For starters, we have to know what mindfulness is, not by learning definitions of mindfulness (although they can help), but by knowing the experience of it. The most accessible way to begin to experience mindfulness is through practicing meditation.

Meditation and Mindfulness

Although "mindfulness" and "meditation" have received lots of attention lately in the media, in academia, and in professional trainings, these words can be mysterious. One reason is that so many different kinds of activity are called "meditation." These range from mulling over a particular topic or situation (as when asked to "meditate on it"), to attaining some exalted or altered state of consciousness. Another reason is that meditation and mindfulness both involve direct experience, not theory, so that until a person actually engages in them, it's difficult to know what they are.

Mindfulness and meditation, although overlapping, are not synonymous. Mindfulness is a condition, and meditation is a technique for cultivating it. Mindfulness is the state or condition of being aware of one's experience in a simple, relaxed way. The type of meditation this book suggests is the practice of being aware of whatever arises in our minds and in our perceptions; in other words, when we meditate, we practice being present and mindful. In this way meditation cultivates mindfulness. Cultivating mindfulness in a formal meditation practice helps us build our mindfulness "muscles," creating the psychological counterpart to muscle memory, which in turn naturally increases mindfulness in other activities.

This book sometimes uses the two terms together, as in "mindfulness meditation," but even when the "mindfulness" qualifier is left off, that's the kind of meditation this book is about. Through this practice we harness our wayward attention spans, allowing us to be present in our lives more fully. As we become more directly engaged in our life experience, we can accomplish our objectives in more fulfilling ways.

Meditation Is Different

Nobody practicing meditation for the first time knows exactly what they're getting into, even if they've read a lot about it before trying it. We may know intellectually that meditation involves working with habitual patterns, emotions, and thoughts; nevertheless, taking that first step can feel like leaping into the unknown. It's a big shift to move from intellectual concepts to the experience itself.

I learned that when I began meditating. Understanding what mindfulness is only comes with experience and familiarity. Once we cultivate it, we find that it's a completely natural human experience; it allows us to see things simply, as they are, rather than through the filters of our particular take, or slant, or spin. With mindfulness we encounter ourselves on a basic level, a level that both includes personal interpretation and also transcends it, giving us more direct access to the experience of whatever we encounter.

The basic state cultivated in mindfulness meditation is called by different names in various traditions. Although in this book I'll simply call it "presence," we could call it "awareness," or our "basic state of being," or our "basic nature," or "basic goodness" (Chögyam Trungpa's term); but the terminology itself isn't so important. As we familiarize ourselves through practice, the experience itself takes the foreground.

Although the simplest way to encounter presence is by meditation practice, this doesn't mean that presence can *only* be experienced through meditating. After all, presence is a completely natural human experience we all have from time to time, especially in moments of great beauty, shock, delight, or sadness. The difference is that in meditation we deliberately cultivate our capacity to notice—and eventually rest in—simple presence. We also notice how we get distracted by thoughts and emotions.

Over the past few years, I've had the opportunity to lead programs, retreats, and trainings for people in a variety of businesses and professions, introducing the participants to mindfulness meditation. For most it was a new experience; nevertheless, perhaps because professional people—lawyers, executives, artists, therapists, teachers, and others—already appreciate the benefits of discipline due to the nature of their work, they often readily connect with mindfulness meditation. They see the value of being present instead of lost in their thoughts. Nobody has ever told me, "I'd rather zone out."

How Does Meditation Work?

Once we realize how the untrained mind fails to connect fully with the world, the benefits of applying mindfulness become apparent. As we start observing our minds, we see how the untrained mind separates us from our direct experience by automatically and relentlessly accompanying our experience with mental and emotional commentary. That commentary colors our experience and distracts us from being present with what is happening around us.

Imagine being so busy planning a rebuttal to an imagined slight in a opponent's presentation that you miss his main point, or avoiding an overly chatty subordinate only to find out later that she took her money-earning idea to your boss. How about being in the middle of a presentation and seeing a look on your superior's face that causes you to lose confidence in what you're saying and sputter to a close, never knowing that his expression was triggered by remembering he'd forgotten to make dinner reservations? In situations like these, our inner dialogue actually harms our perception of reality, as its filter of interpretation colors our experience. The inner commentary is so ubiquitous and has been with us so long that we don't even realize it's there, much less that there is an alternative.

Mindfulness meditation helps us drop the habitual sound track. While sitting in meditation, we begin to notice that not only do we have thoughts, but they are often repetitive. And not only are they repetitive, they often have nothing to do with anything that's actually going on around us. Habitual mental chatter is like leaving the TV on without watching it, creating meaningless background noise. Conversely, the experience of presence is like watching a sporting event on TV without the commentary or "color"—or even better, attending the event in person, where we can feel the energy of the crowd and hear the sounds of the game. Once we see how our inner chatter resembles the endless repetitions of a dotty old uncle, we find it less convincing. We don't need to take it so seriously.

Meditation also shows us that there is an alternative to habitual inner turmoil, something that is true, consistent, and accessible. It is that sense of presence, of just being here, in a body, with sense perceptions, both external and internal. Presence is so simple and so subtle that we may have missed it for most of our lives, or only noticed it peeking through in moments of tenderness or beauty. Meditation lets us notice simple presence and see that it's always there behind the mental chatter, an ever-present screen on which our sense perceptions and other experiences are projected.

Presence is what hears our thoughts, feels our emotions, and perceives our experiences. When we learn to rest in presence, not only do we inhabit our lives more fully, we bring greater enthusiasm and insight to every aspect of life. Contrary to the idea that meditation is for self-absorbed navel-gazers, we find that its practice helps us engage more fully with whatever life offers.

The mindfulness cultivated by meditation opens us to creative solutions and insights so that we can be more skillful in work and relationships with others. When we are in the midst of a constant storm of thoughts, some of which may include valuable information, it's hard to tell the wheat from the chaff. Slowing down the distractedness of mind is like panning for gold: it allows innovative ideas to reveal themselves as the treasures they are.

Life is Full of Surprises

During the months of writing this book, the challenges I faced were the usual ones facing any writer. Am I making sense? Does the book's logic lead where I want it to? Will readers find it engaging? It was only after completing the first draft that a new challenge presented itself: I was diagnosed with lung cancer. This was a new experience for me: other than childhood asthma, I had been blessed by having few grave health challenges.

Suddenly mortality was staring me in the face. Not that I hadn't been aware of the terminal aspect of our human condition; after all, I had been exposed to Buddhism for decades, and the Buddhists make no secret of it. But until now it had been a future likelihood, not a potentially current fact. So I thought to myself, OK, fella, it's one thing to talk a good game of mindfulness, but let's see how you do with this!

The doctors were initially quite optimistic about the speed of my recovery from the removal of my lung. That was before the complications began, complications that would bring me very near to death more than once; they led to several months of hospitalization (and a second surgery to deal with infection) plus more months of gradual recovery at home, giving me plenty of time and opportunity to explore my relationship to mindfulness.

While I wasn't back out on the golf course in a month as the surgeon had predicted, it was nevertheless, satisfying to discover that, yes, the basic sense of presence was still readily accessible. And when thoughts of the "why me?" variety arose, they were strangely uncompelling. Even the feeling of fear, although sometimes present, was not overwhelming. (My wife tells a different story about fear during that time, but she too found mindfulness to be her most reliable ally.)

If anything, the experience of encountering mortality was strangely reassuring: Yes, this mindfulness actually *does* work; it's not just a comforting philosophy. The silver lining of my health crisis is that it gave me further confidence in presenting this book because I know, on a very basic and personal level, the inner advantage that applying mindfulness brings.

How to Use This Book

The first part of this book, "The Added Value of Presence," explores the state of presence—how to recognize it, become familiar with it, and develop confidence in our ability to connect with it. Once we get the knack of relaxing into presence, we can do it with genuine confidence and humor. Even if we're nervous, presence makes it easier to meet the challenges of our professional activities because when we are actually present with them, we perceive them more accurately.

In addition to learning to recognize distraction, as we cultivate mindfulness we begin to notice how fear and nervousness often arise when we are challenged to perform at a high level of competence. Therefore, Part Two, "Fear: The Untapped Asset," examines the many forms fear can take, how our avoidance of it helps to fuel our inner commentary, and how we can harness its energy. Even the most confident and accomplished people experience the energy or "feel" of nervousness that this book calls the "fear feeling." Musicians and actors may call it stage fright but the experience is not limited to performers.

At the beginning of Part Three, our emphasis shifts from basic mindfulness techniques to the specifics of how mindfulness can be applied in ordinary life and work situations. This focuses initially on decision-making because decisions are a part of so many of our activities, both at work and elsewhere; it also illustrates how the ability to remain undistracted and to relate with fear mindfully can give us an advantage in all kinds of situations.

We continue this shift of focus further in Part Three by dealing with activities professionals face every day and discussing how to apply mindfulness and the skills and insights that arise from cultivating it. Drawing on my own experience and that of others, this section explores communication, diplomacy, negotiation, creativity, intuition, collaboration, encouraging excellence, and leadership.

The last section of the book, "Mindfulness Dividends," is about how the strengths (mindfulness muscles) that are cultivated by training in mindfulness spill over into other parts of our lives.

At the end of the book are several appendices designed to help you cultivate mindfulness in a variety of situations.

The first summarizes briefly the mindfulness meditation technique that is recommended in this book and described at the beginning of Part One.

The second is an overview of the fear practice which is examined in detail in Part Two of the book. This appendix offers a point-by-point review to make it easy to remember.

The third appendix summarizes the contemplation practice that is described more fully in the discussion of decision-making in Part Three.

The fourth appendix describes a number of exercises you can do on your own to help make mindful presence even more familiar and available, so you can apply it in a multitude of situations.

The fifth appendix lists further readings you may find helpful.

1

The Added Value
of Presence

How to Practice Mindfulness Meditation

There are many practices called "meditation," and the style of each reflects what the practice is intended to accomplish. The meditation practice presented in this book is intended to cultivate your innate sense of presence or, if described as a corrective, to help you become less distracted.

It can be challenging for one beginning the practice to have confidence that he or she is doing it "correctly." So, if you're trying this on your own, you might want to have a conversation with someone who is more experienced in meditation done in this way, since that can help avoid sidetracks. If you don't know such a person, by all means do the practice on your own; however, if you find yourself engaged in a lot of theorizing about the practice, try to let that go and come back to the simple experience of being present.

Also, if you find (as you will) that you have lots of thoughts, don't be discouraged; it's a natural part of the experience. Just remember, you're not trying to get rid of the thoughts—an impossibility, other than perhaps momentarily—but to become familiar with them so that, over time, they interfere less with being present.

The practice begins with finding a quiet place where you can be undisturbed for a little while and then finding a comfortable seat there. It can be a meditation cushion, a chair, or a bench, whichever is available to you.

Before you start, decide how long you want your meditation session to last. It doesn't have to be a long time, but it helps to decide in advance. You may want to use a timer so you don't have to keep checking the time. If this is your first time, try five or ten minutes.

Next, take a comfortable posture in which you can sit upright but not tense, like a column that supports itself. It can be helpful to make sure your knees are below your hip joints to reduce tension in your muscles. The easiest way to do this is to sit forward on your seat so that your legs naturally fall below your hips. Just be sure your seat is high enough to allow this. You don't need to adopt a fancy posture; just find one that's reasonably comfortable. As your session continues, don't be afraid to adjust your posture so you can be more comfortable and relaxed. Sitting this way is not something most of us have done a lot, since we mostly lean against the back of the furniture we're sitting on. Just remember to sit forward to keep your knees low.

Once your posture is established, rest your hands on your thighs or fold them in your lap, whatever feels better to you. You don't have to do this the same way every time. No elaborate hand positions are recommended.

Keep your eyes open and relax your gaze, without trying to focus on a particular spot or object. Let your gaze rest downward, a short distance in front of you, and let it take in whatever is in your field of vision.

Having taken your seat in this way, simply notice the experience of being a person, in a body, with sense perceptions. You see whatever is in your field of vision. You hear whatever sounds register in your ears; they can come from traffic outdoors, bird songs, or a nearby appliance. Your sense of touch may register the coolness or warmth of the air, the feeling of your seat against the cushion, chair, or bench you're sitting on, the touch of your clothing against your skin. You may smell aromas in your environment. Notice that these all happen at the same time: you don't have to switch your perceptions on—they happen naturally.

Notice your breathing, which you'll experience as a sense perception: you may feel the air moving in and out of your nose or mouth, or you may hear it, or you may feel the rising and falling of your torso as you breathe, or you may experience some combination of the three. Just treat the breathing as another of your perceptions, along with the other senses.

Similarly you will experience bodily sensations, whether as muscle tension or the weight of your hands on your thighs or lap, or the feeling of your shoulders suspended from your collarbones.

Notice also that all these happen at the same time. You hear and smell while you're seeing; you feel your breath at the same time you're noticing other physical sensations and seeing what's in front of you. Keep it simple; don't overcomplicate it by trying to catalog the sense experiences, both outer and inner. They happen very naturally, all at once. Just let the unitary experience of presence happen.

As you sit in meditation, you'll inevitably notice that you've gotten caught up in thinking. When that happens, simply come back to the experience of being present with sense perceptions, bodily sensations, and breathing—until you notice again that you've been distracted by your thinking. Just do this over and over.

You may feel that you've spent most of the time caught up in thoughts, with very little time spent simply being present. That's okay; it's just part of the process of gradually undermining the habitual quality of continual thinking.

If you like, you can add a technique called "labeling." To do this, when you notice that you've been caught in thinking, just label it "thinking," that is, think the word "thinking" and then go back to the experience of being present. Labeling doesn't mean classifying your thoughts as good, exciting, repulsive, or indifferent; it's merely highlighting to yourself that thinking has occurred. Simply acknowledge thoughts as "thinking" and return to being present. If we try to classify the thoughts, we're just adding more thinking to the meditation process. So just keep it simple: be present, notice when you've been caught in your thoughts, label them "thinking," and go back to being present.

There are times when it is useful to look at the quality of your thoughts, as you begin to learn to recognize the mindset your thoughts create for you; however, this is a different activity—more along the lines of contemplation, which is described later in this book—not the simple process of meditation. There's nothing wrong with it; just don't consider it a substitute for meditation.

To sum up, the three main parts of meditation practice involve:

❖ *taking a comfortable, alert posture;*
❖ *noticing the experience of being present;*
❖ *returning to the experience of presence after you notice that you've been caught up in your thoughts.*
❖ *The optional fourth part is to label thoughts "thinking."*

Do this over and over for the time you've committed to meditating. Be clear with yourself about how long you're going to sit in meditation, and stick to it.

Particularly at first, the experience can be uncomfortable, especially because of its thought-filled quality; but this is the way that you familiarize yourself with how your mind works. Lots of people have done this, and you can, too.

It is the very simplicity of this practice that makes it so powerful: you don't distract yourself with theorizing but allow yourself to notice the experience of presence in a very basic way. This is how you become familiar with the ground from which you can experience every part of your life.

Getting Started

As I discovered long ago meditating in Vermont, one of the first things people notice when they begin this practice is how many thoughts they have. If they keep at it, they also start to recognize that there is a distinction between their thoughts and the "reality" the thoughts purport to describe. This is a powerful insight: thoughts offer only a particular perspective about, or interpretation of, what is going on. Rather than being a reliable tool for relating to challenges in our lives, the conceptual or thought-centered mind is fickle. What attracts us one day may repel us the next, or leave us completely unmoved.

So instead of pledging allegiance to our fickle minds, believing whatever we happen to think at the moment and backpedaling when our opinions shift, mindfulness offers an alternative—just relax into the simple experience of presence. At the beginning, presence may seem elusive, crowded out by the blur of thinking, but that's everybody's starting point. Presence is always available and reliable; you just have to notice it.

One of the ways we notice is that, as we continue meditating, we begin to experience that there are gaps in our thinking, gaps where nothing seems to be happening. When we notice those gaps over and over, we start to appreciate that they're not "nothing," but actually represent glimpses of presence. Although they may seem at first like transitory interruptions in our thinking, as they become more familiar, we realize that the gaps of presence are the norm. Our thinking, at least the habitual, churning thoughts, is the interruption. We can relax with both the gaps and the thoughts and let natural presence reveal itself more and more.

"Mind the Gap." For over forty years this slogan has been posted in the London Underground. It has become famous and can be found emblazoned on coffee mugs, tee shirts, and bumper stickers. It's good advice that, as this book will illustrate, goes way beyond railway safety.

Recognizing Presence

A parable of presence: two young fish are swimming along together in a pond when an old fish approaches from the opposite direction. As the old fish passes he remarks, "How's the water today, fellas?" The youngsters keep on swimming, and then one turns to the other: "What's water?"

Presence is like water. And, like the young fish, we may never have noticed the simple experience of presence. Recognizing it begins with acknowledging that we may never have considered whether we're present or not. Until someone flags the issue for us, we might not even think about it.

I've sometimes entered business and social situations shrouded in a mental chatter of strategies about what I was going to do, what I was going to say. The result was a sense of pressure, as I tried to enter the situation while simultaneously attempting to recall my agenda. Of course, we do go into certain situations only because there *is* a strategy to be executed, some reason for being there. But our inner chatter about the strategy obscures our connection with the situation. If we don't know how to rest in presence, we're stuck in the noise of mental chatter. It's like being in a room where too many voices make it difficult to hear.

Such inner noise is not only stressful, it's counterproductive. The effect of that constant haze of mental chatter is either to mask or filter our experience, or to distract us. It's comparable to the difference between looking directly at a flower and focusing on its color, its smell, and its freshness, or doing the same thing while trying to recall the genus or species of the plant. The same thing can happen in a business negotiation session, when being in the mental haze of your strategies may cause you to miss subtle cues that could be productive. The alternative to cloaking yourself in that haze is to enter each situation connected to a simple sense of presence.

But first you have to know that presence is a possibility.

Presence is the state or condition people are in when they are not distracted. In presence we experience our sense perceptions, bodily aches and pains, and emotions or feelings. We also experience what is around us more directly. Although presence is innate, most of us need meditation and other mindfulness disciplines to cultivate it. The operative word is "cultivate." Presence is not something that we acquire, nor is it something *caused* by meditation or mindfulness.

In fact, it seems to be the other way around; we can practice mindfulness and meditation precisely because presence is already there as a basic part of our human equipment.

When we cultivate presence we uncover the ability to inhabit our lives fully. In other words, we're not just going through the motions of a life as described and accompanied by the narrative commentary in our heads. Instead, we're discovering how to live as openly and completely as possible. Recognizing both the experience of presence as well as its application in the rest of our lives, we learn to be more fully who we are, to manifest presence. Then we are able to live our lives as an expression of presence, connected to the ground of presence that is always available.

Applied Mindfulness

Our term for this cultivated skill is "applied mindfulness." Presence and applied mindfulness are not two separate conditions. When we cultivate one, we cultivate the other; the more we cultivate a state of presence, the more we apply mindfulness. Likewise, by applying mindfulness in everyday situations, we expand the experience of presence into a broader arena, making it even more available.

Through meditation we heighten our awareness about the workings of our minds. Sitting meditation allows its practitioners to notice both the fog of getting wrapped up in one's own thinking as well as the moments of presence when the thinking is interrupted. When we take that awareness into our everyday lives, we may find ourselves noticing when we've zoned out in the midst of a conversation. And at the very moment we notice we've been distracted, we are back in the state of presence—at least until we start generating further mental chatter.

For beginning meditators, the mental commentary often includes negative thoughts about being distracted—as if you've done something wrong; however, as you become more experienced, you'll realize that such fault-finding thoughts are just another form of distraction. You don't have to validate them by believing them and flagellating yourself. You can let those thoughts go too.

The alternation of distraction and presence is not fundamentally different in daily living from that experienced in meditation; however, the alternation is highlighted vividly in meditation because of the starkness of sitting doing "nothing." Sitting meditation allows you to see the difference clearly because there are no other activities going on to confuse the issue. You can recognize the distraction of habitual thinking that accompanies your activities like a soundtrack. As a result, the alternation becomes more obvious in everyday life and highlights the application of presence to ongoing life situations. Seeing the alternation between distraction and presence clues you into the difference between thoughts and reality, the map and the terrain.

Another thing people begin to notice is how identifying with your thoughts creates challenges in everyday life. You identify with them because you see them as an integral part of yourself; they feel familiar and personal. If anyone challenges your thoughts, you feel challenged personally. But as you sit in meditation, where you also initially identify with your thoughts, you begin to see their shifting and fickle quality. This makes it easier to dis-identify with them.

In everyday life situations, where thoughts and perceptions can seem like a consolidated experience, rather than one being a commentary on the other, you may tend to give your thoughts the same credence as words someone has spoken to you or a look you noticed on someone's face. You see them as real.

As a result you may notice that, although thoughts may be easier to recognize while sitting, untangling that web is harder in post-meditation. This is no reason for discouragement. It's just how it works. Even beginning to notice the alternation between distraction and presence in post-meditation indicates heightened awareness.

Avoiding "Near-Life" Experience

The state of presence that arises when people apply mindfulness is often called "genuineness" or "authenticity." Through mindfulness meditation you consciously choose to cultivate that condition, to trust yourself as a real person, as you actually are, and not as a fragmentary version of yourself, conforming to a self-image.

Before experiencing and recognizing presence, our conceptual chatter describes, analyzes, and evaluates our feelings, so that we assume and believe that the chatter itself is an integral part of the feelings. But when we settle into presence through meditation, we experience something more fundamental: who we truly are and how we really feel, not merely a self-image constructed with our thoughts. Confronting situations, we start to realize that our responses do not have to be limited to what we think but can arise from the simple presence we've cultivated, as well as from bodily sensations that offer another level of insight about our response. As the

experience of presence becomes more familiar and trustworthy, we realize that it's possible to live life in the moment.

It's very simple; there is nothing grandiose about it. Nobody is likely to think you're a hero because of it, but you'll
feel like you're really living your life and not just having a
conversation with yourself about it. You will have traded
"near-life" experience for the real thing, living genuinely
rather than in a story you're telling yourself.

Mindful Living: Genuineness, Equanimity, and Clarity

Living genuinely avoids one of the often unacknowledged
pitfalls of life—deception. When we try to mask part of
ourselves or cover up a mistake with excuses or finger-point-
ing, we create complications. These may require yet other
strategic solutions, not to mention the fact that such behavior
can create hard feelings and the sense in others that we are
not quite straightforward.

Who doesn't know the experience of unexpectedly being
asked "Is something bothering you?" and replying "Oh, no,
it's nothing," either because we don't know ourselves what is
going on within us, or we don't want to admit it. If you don't
recognize what you are unconsciously communicating to
those around you, or don't want to acknowledge it, you often
end up saying something that's simply not true. Or it could
be that it's something that you haven't even been willing to
admit to yourself.

So we come to appreciate deception's two sides. One is
misleading others, but most of us are not deliberate liars, so
the deception that arises with respect to other people is often
a result of mindlessly attempting to avoid discomfort. We frequently rationalize such behavior as a harmless "white lie."
Practicing mindfulness, you have a chance to boycott this and

other such habits, not by blurting everything out, but by getting over the feeling that you have to react immediately to an arising situation. Before the space of presence provides us with other options, we tend to react in whatever way is most comfortable, a habitual reaction pulled out of our bag of tricks. Becoming familiar with presence, we gain options allowing us to slow down and respond with more care and deliberation.

The other side of deception is how we deceive ourselves. Self-deception works unconsciously, or it doesn't work. Once you become aware of deceiving yourself, the game is up, and self-deception becomes nonfunctional. If you tell another person something you don't believe is true, they may or may not detect your deception; when self-deception becomes shaky, however, our tendency is often to dig in harder, trying to reinforce our habitual story.

Mindfulness makes that form of denial more difficult to accomplish. Becoming more familiar with our thoughts and emotions, we recognize them as distinct from tangible reality; thus, as we practice mindfulness we slow down enough to see our habitual perspective and, rather than being something to take for granted, we can question whether it is the whole story or whether we are trying to fool ourselves. Seeing through self-deception also helps avoid deceiving others, because we can slow ourselves down enough to respond from a place of presence and authenticity.

What can be said about living in presence this way? When we rely on our thoughts rather than the state of presence, we often behave with what seems like mandatory reactivity. We feel that whatever happens calls for a response, requiring that we have some opinion or view about it, or that we take some action pronto. A mindful person, rather than getting all caught up in and wrought up by a situation, will simply notice it, let it be what is, and stay present while considering the best course of action.

Manifesting from the ground of presence, we discover the possibility of genuine equanimity in any situation. We don't have to panic, or jump the gun. We can connect with our experience, not by smoothing things over or immediately trying to fix them, but by connecting with what's happening completely and simply. Instead of getting all worked up, wondering, "What am I going to do now? Gotta do something about that!" we learn to keep our balance while remaining completely connected to the situation.

As equanimity begins to pervade our presence, our demeanor becomes decent and reasonable. If we don't know the solution to a problem, we can simply say so, and that we'll look into it further. When we jettison our unacknowledged agendas by resting in presence, we don't need to make something out of a charged situation. We don't freak out, shut down, or react explosively. We're just there with it. We're genuine about it, with no need to claim that we had a different response to it than we did.

In mindful experience, there is a continual alternation between *resting* receptively in presence and *engaging* in activity while staying connected with presence. This is different from the earlier alternation between presence and habitual patterns. As presence becomes more reliably accessible, there is no need to avoid engaging with life situations fully; rather you can maintain the connection with presence and at the same time think, speak, and act, bringing mindfulness into every activity.

This opens you up to greater possibilities. Because your mind is not continually generating chatter, you will have more clarity about experience. You will simply see, hear, and feel, without filtering experience through a habitual mindset, connecting instead through your perceptions. Your senses all work just fine (unless you have a disability); you hear, see, taste, smell, touch, and feel, and you do these automatically.

Learning to trust this brings a sense of completeness and connection in all your activities.

Seeing things, people, and situations more clearly, your experience becomes more vivid. Colors will become brighter, the sound of a person's voice more distinct. Experiences will feel very close to you because you're not always taking a step back, separating yourself from them with habitual mental patterns such as, "What do I think about that? What do I think about that person's voice? What do I think about the way that person looks? What do I think about the temperature in the room?"

We can trust our natural responses to that vivid experience. Whether your heart is touched by a person or situation, whether you have a sense of sadness, or delight, or irritation, will depend on the circumstances, but something does happen within you when you don't have lots of thoughts to defend. And the fact that something might go wrong is not always a big deal—although sometimes it is. Still, things are just what they are. Sometimes they go the way you want, and sometimes they don't.

When our minds are completely filled with a stream of chatter, it is harder to distinguish the good from the bad; however, if our psychological space is not consumed by thoughts, then when responses occur, we can entertain the question of whether there is merit to them.

The experience that arises from presence is open-hearted and vivid in terms of perceptions, and spacious and humorous in terms of state of mind. In that state, you begin to have a different attitude toward your responses. As a kind of post-meditation practice, you can observe your own responses as phenomena to witness rather than feeling obligated to identify with them. Instead of automatically identifying with or building a story line around your responses, an uncluttered mind allows you to see responses as a way of expressing wisdom or intelligence about the situation—something positive or beneficial you can contribute.

Is There a Problem?

I remember having, before I first learned to meditate, the experience of some phrase repeating in my head. I don't remember what it was, only that it was annoying and I wondered what was going on. The notion that it might be obscuring my experience of presence never occurred to me. It was only after my experience of meditating at the center in Vermont that, like a fish finally noticing the water, I had my first glimpse of presence.

I was heading out for a few days of backpacking on the Appalachian Trail in New Hampshire after my time at the meditation center. Waiting for the Greyhound bus in the village where I was staying, I went into the general store for some peanuts and crackers. I came back out, walked over to the stop sign where I had propped my backpack, and looked out over the Connecticut River Valley.

All at once I was engulfed in the sensation of vast open space; there was nothing going on but my own sensory perceptions. I had never had an experience like that before. It was impressive—so impressive that I immediately started thinking about it and—surprise, surprise—the experience dissipated, and I was back in my thoughts, wondering what happened. What was that experience? And why had I never had it before?

In retrospect, I realize those questions are at the heart of the issue. Why is that? Why do people space out so much— getting lost in their thoughts— instead of just being present?

One of the most significant reasons is the power of habit. We have been relying upon our thoughts for a very long time—most of our lives to be exact. Early on when we begin to differentiate ourselves from our parents, we start to apply conceptual structures to understand the world we are in. The first ones are very basic—self and other. Then we move on to more elaborate constructs—how to perform certain functions, starting with little childhood games and progressing as we learn how to get what we want. Crying may work for a while, but it eventually loses its effectiveness; we begin to learn how to reason and explain. We discard strategies that don't work so well and retain the reliable ones until they reach their shelf life.

This simplified description of the developmental process paints the picture of human beings as toolmakers, using what works and discarding the rest. Although scientific studies indicate that we are not as rational as we'd like to believe, even if that's true—that we make up our minds on a subconscious level before we decide consciously—we can nevertheless still observe the difference between fixating on thoughts and simply being present with what we're experiencing in the moment, and so break the habit that binds us to distraction.

There's another reason presence may go unnoticed: it's quiet. Other mental contents are so much louder: vivid thoughts and emotions are impressive and take up a lot of mental space. Simple presence is like a mirror reflecting what's going on without drawing attention to itself. Compared to the vividness of compelling thoughts and hot emotions, presence may seem like nothing at all. So to level the playing field between the vivid mental contents and simple presence, it helps if someone says, about presence, "Notice the mirror. It's worth paying attention to. Something happens when you do."

Another reason some people don't connect with presence is that they don't believe they have the potential to change. Even when things are going badly, creating lots of unpleasantness in their own lives and the lives of the people around them, they think there's no alternative, no hope for relief. That can be a tough assumption to overcome, but neuroscience tells us that the notion of an unchangeable brain is incorrect, and that brain changes correlate with changes in emotional and attentive states. They call this phenomenon "neuroplasticity." Our mental patterns are like paths worn through a grassy lawn; new paths can be found by walking elsewhere than on the old ones. By shifting your attention from fixation on thoughts to paying attention to presence, you can start to open new pathways.

Another obstacle, especially for accomplished professionals, is the preconception that making money is inconsistent with meditative and contemplative practice, that all that "soft stuff" gets in the way of the bottom line. Other people automatically associate money with attachment, greed, and aggression, believing wealth to be responsible for these tortuous and destructive emotions. There are many ways to complicate the relationship between earning a living and developing a contemplative life.

But money is just another kind of energy; economic incentives are just another kind of karma (karma simply meaning the laws of cause and effect); and the way you relate to all that is what makes the difference: are you relating to financial energy in a mindful way or through a web of habitual patterns and assumptions? Especially in the world of applied mindfulness this is a fertile subject for contemplation. Opening up to your world involves looking at the many ways you relate to money—and other aspects of life—uncovering your assumptions and preconceptions, especially the unacknowledged ones.

Recognizing the Sticky Bits

Unless we acknowledge that presence is real, meaningful, and worth addressing, it's hard to connect with it. Sometimes the challenge arises from people having intertwined their stream of thoughts so deeply with simple sensory experience that the possibility of seeing them as separate phenomena never arises. In other words, they've identified thoughts with experience so thoroughly that they think the thoughts are the experience. That identification can also apply to how we view ourselves. We see ourselves as the "I" in the narrative, "I'm here. See?" Or Descartes's famous non sequitur, "I think, therefore I am."

The difficulty arises from equating our personal commentary with what we are experiencing. We don't see the commentary as something separate, perhaps triggered by, but nevertheless an unreliable narrator of, what's going on around us. We see a coworker and automatically affix a story line to him or her as "good guy or gal," "jerk," "undermining enemy," "threatening boss." And this commentary often involves more than simply tagging someone with a concept or name. It can also have an emotional component, sometimes referred to as "getting your buttons pushed," and being expressed as annoyance, irritation, or anger. Then the habitual mental tendency is to construct a story line about the other person or event: "He enjoys trying to make it difficult for me;" or "She's trying to take my job;" or "I hate situations like this." As we move from a simple label to a narrative and string these narratives together, broad interpretations or explanations emerge. Collections of these create a mindset through which future experiences are filtered.

Using these narratives to "make sense" of life can help what happens around us feel less disjointed and give us a sense of being in control. This creates a comfort zone which, even though it exists only in our own heads, seems reassuring. Because this experience of comfort appeals to us more than the uncertainty and randomness that so often permeate the conditions in life, we find ourselves creating such narratives over and over, until the stories start to seem like reality itself. Thus we mentally create the context in which we experience things and people. The plot thickens, literally.

In addition to these reflexes of thought, feeling, emotion, and narrative, our habitual mind sandbags us further by clinging to its sense of identification with our reactions. Reactions are not images neutrally projected on a screen; rather, we have a personal investment in seeing them as important. I remember seeing a bumper sticker that said, "If you're not outraged, you're not paying attention!" That pretty much sums up this pattern—your outrage confirms your sense of being a person who notices and cares. It even creates an implicit obligation to stay angry because if you don't, you're a person who doesn't care. Quite a responsibility!

Of course, not all expressions of identification are so heated. Nevertheless, adopting them ourselves makes them special to us, almost as if we own them. Self-identification occurs when people select, consciously or otherwise, a particular pattern to identify with. It might be the idea that I am a "responsible person," "a compassionate person," a "go-to guy or gal", a "tough cookie," a "realist," or the like.

If you ask someone what kind of person he or she is, the answer usually comes from this level. And it can be unsettling for a person who has a firmly held self-image to manifest thoughts or behaviors inconsistent with that image. ("I don't know what came over me!" Or the turtle defense, "I just snapped!") Even though we probably wouldn't consciously consider these narratives as something we invented (after all, that would defeat the purpose of seeing them as real), identifying with them gives us a sense of personal specialness.

A few years ago I gave a talk about meditation. I was sitting in a chair and wearing a jacket and tie. During the Q&A following the talk, a fellow at the back of the room shot his hand up and said, "I can't learn anything from somebody who wears a tie!"

I was surprised and somewhat amused, as were many other people in the room. But he wasn't joking, as his tone of voice confirmed. I don't imagine he thought of himself as a closed-minded person; his objection to a tie probably arose from an assumption that ties symbolize authority or hierarchy and the narrowness and rigidity sometimes associated with them. At the same time, I suspected his challenge to me reflected a rigidity that was probably inconsistent with his self-image.

Keep in mind that the story lines we occupy ourselves with aren't necessarily false. Indeed, they are even more powerful if they are credible. The point about story lines is that they become the subject matter of distraction, and that keeps us from being present and engaged with whatever realities we're relating to. So, two apparently conflicting statements—"That's just a story line" and "It's true!"—aren't inconsistent at all, at least not from this perspective.

The Meditative Perspective

Mindfulness meditation provides a way to unwind these patterns. Observing mental events arising, whether as thoughts, emotions, story lines, bodily sensations, or daydreams, the mindfulness practitioner becomes familiar with them and their patterns. Meditators frequently notice a repetitive quality to their thoughts (hence the references throughout this book to "habitual patterns").

They may also notice the inconsistent character or quality of these contents, and how their minds seem to bounce randomly from one topic to another, a phenomenon known as "discursiveness." Noticing this through mindfulness meditation, a person begins to become familiar with the lay of the mental and emotional landscape. Deliberately boycotting the impulse to evaluate (positively or negatively), change, or reject these contents, the mindfulness practitioner learns to see them merely as something that arises, hangs around for a bit, and then dissolves, like the weather or passing scenery.

This perspective undermines the tendency to identify with the contents of mind, to see the contents as oneself, or even as an integral part of oneself. If contents are repetitive and often unrelated to what's really going on, why should we take them seriously? If thoughts are inconsistent—liking something at one moment, disliking it the next—how can they form the basis of being a genuine person? If my thoughts are discursive and I identify with them, does that make me just a grab bag of tendencies?

Seeing thoughts and narratives as a part of ourselves causes us to feel the need to defend or justify them; after all, if those thoughts are me (or a valued part of me) and they're flawed, conflicted, or incoherent, then obviously I have a problem. From the meditative perspective, we can easily see why stress, irritation, and other uncomfortable states result from trying to identify with something so messy.

Any time we start a new activity, we may feel defensive about it. Why are we making that change? For example, as I mentioned, when I first meditated I had recurring thoughts about how to explain my activities to people back home who had no experience of it. I really felt a need to justify my activities to them, even though nobody was asking me to. However, I was unwilling or unable to connect to those feelings in terms of self-justification, so I did my habitual thing, which was to generate irritable thoughts, thus shifting responsibility from my own inner doubt to annoyance with what somebody "out there" was inflicting on me – my law partners, who wouldn't understand what I was doing, or the timekeeper who waited so long to close the session with a gong. Pretty handy, huh?

Another problem with habitual patterns is that they usually involve interpreting your experience in terms of the past or the future, not the present; whereas resting in presence opens you up and allows your awareness to arise freely as relaxed alertness—yet another description of mindfulness.

Just to clarify: although I talk about habitual mind as a phenomenon, it's not really separate from you. And although you often identify with it, it's not really who you are either. Once you gain perspective on your thinking process, you begin to see that these habitual patterns flow in and out of your life experience. Sometimes they are like a tape loop or broken record, repeating over and over. At other times they are completely inconsistent and helter-skelter. That's just mental activity doing what it does. It only becomes a problem when you identify with the whole thing as "me."

Coming into the Present

Meditation practice, while not a cure-all, is an incredibly valuable tool for perceiving mental contents and the experience of presence; however, especially when beginning to practice mindfulness meditation, it helps to remember that all the old patterns are still in full swing. The habitual thinking process, as we begin to sit in meditation, still commands center stage.

One of the classic laments of beginning meditators is, "I have so many thoughts. It's discouraging." And it is true that once we have an intellectual understanding of how we've overvalued our thoughts, it's easy to feel discouraged when those thoughts are taking up so much experiential space; however, this perception, rather than being a problem, is itself a significant insight: we are seeing our overvaluation of and habituation to the thinking process in full relief. It may not feel comfortable, but it's a good thing in the long run. We learn about our minds empirically by observing them in action.

There are a couple of classic (and erroneous) responses to overvaluation of our thoughts. One is to become fascinated with the thinking process as a phenomenon to be explored. Of course, this isn't all bad, since it can undermine identification with the thinking process. However, expounding on all of one's habitual patterns can also become a credential for how perceptive one has become through meditation, a more refined form of self-praise. (Overvaluation of thoughts may reflect an impulse to avoid boredom; after all, with the thinking process so prominent, it may seem to be where the action is.)

The other classic response is to believe that the goal is to rid ourselves of our thoughts. This happens even though, in the tradition in which I trained, meditation instructors emphasize that getting rid of thoughts is *not* the point. And even though that point is repeated, repeatedly. Perhaps novices are just spaced out when that instruction is given, or maybe they reflect a prevalent either-or mentality that finds it difficult to grasp that the truth is somewhere in the middle. As a friend of mine once said to a meditation class, "If you were supposed to get rid of your thoughts, we would have told you."

So although we are not trying to rid ourselves of thoughts, we do become aware that exclusive reliance on them in living our lives is like building a house on sand, without a foundation. What's needed is to look deeper to find something reliable and grounding. One approach to this is the illuminating question I heard years ago: "We all know we have thoughts, but what hears your thoughts?"

Approached through meditation, the answer to this question becomes clear: it is the experience we've been describing as presence or awareness. Conceptual mind comes along later (almost instantly!) and comments on the thoughts, but it is simple presence or awareness that sees them first.

We can experience presence most easily while observing our sense perceptions. For example, just look at your hand without analyzing or labeling. That perception is an instance of simple presence. It is on this level that mindfulness occurs; it is what notices the patterns of your thoughts and the quality of your thoughts. It's not necessary to overlay that experience with concepts or story lines; just experience directly what is present.

Once you have recognized simple presence, coming to trust it is a further challenge. You have relied on your thoughts and concepts for so long that if you don't immediately clothe your experience with them, you may feel naked, disoriented, and vulnerable. You may suspect consciously or subconsciously that you won't be able to function without relying on a narrative of thoughts. This is where courage—the ability to relate mindfully with fear—comes in. Abandoning the crutch of familiar patterns is like stepping into the unknown; it actually takes guts, like doing a back flip, jumping off a high dive, or making a speech without notes. Part Two of this book goes into this in more detail.

Discrimination about habits is called for because not all habits are bad; none of us would want to return to the very un-habitual experience we had when first learning to ride a bicycle. Boycotting habitual patterns does *not* mean that we reinvent every wheel, business template, or other useful form—there's actually a lot of wisdom in what people have discovered already.

What it *does* mean is that you approach your work and life with simple presence, and in so doing free up your intelligence to see which of your tools work best. If you are using a template or form simply out of habit, without seeing whether adjustments make sense, you miss out on the potential for creating a higher level of excellence.

The basic equation is this: we are either present or distracted by our habitual patterns. Mindfulness meditation is a
way to cultivate presence and boycott distraction. Learning
to recognize and rest in presence is tremendously valuable
because it opens up the possibility for your innate intelligence, benevolence, and wisdom to arise.

Why Meditation?

People come to meditation for a variety of reasons. Some
see that their dissatisfaction and unhappiness is caused
by negative thoughts about themselves. Others may feel
blocked in their professional or personal lives and hope that
meditation can help them get unstuck. Some experience a lot
of suffering or discomfort, and they may be steered toward
meditation by their therapist or social worker. Life coaches
and business coaches sometimes recommend it. Many people
read about it in magazines or newspapers or hear about it on
TV and wonder whether it has any relevance to them. Some
have learned about meditation through other contemplative
disciplines such as yoga, tai chi, or qigong. And some are just
curious.

Whatever the motivation, it usually involves a sense of
lacking something, that something is missing or incomplete,
that there must be more. Even in the midst of plenty, people
often wonder, what else? The sense of lack is true even with
a motivation as seemingly neutral as curiosity, that there is
something I want to find out. Once some motivation takes
root, then the question becomes, where do I look? Where do
I find something that will be meaningful or useful to me?

Seeking to answer this question, some people turn to
spiritual and religious paths. This book, however, without

opposing any such path, proposes a secular and nonsectarian approach which can actually enhance appreciation of other approaches. Indeed a friend once told me that meditation had infused new meaning into her lifelong cultural tradition, which for her had gotten stale over the years.

The practice of meditation as presented in this book is an essentially human practice, one that gives us the opportunity to explore our innate equipment. We have all been trained, to some extent or other, to use our human equipment; however, for most of us that training will have focused on only certain aspects—frequently the use of conceptual, rational capabilities or physical skills. As my wife says, "We were born with capabilities we don't yet know how to use and what we need is an operator's manual."

An Integrative Process

While certainly not as concrete or handy as a manual might be, mindfulness meditation does give us better access to all our capacities. Through its practice, our awareness opens to our full array of capabilities: conceptual, emotional, communicative, and creative. Because of this, it is an *integrative* approach, allowing all of these aspects to be recognized and appreciated.

The Tibetan lama who introduced me to this approach described it as a continual process of making friends with oneself. When we are motivated to make friends with another person, we want to know who they really are, not merely selected parts of them. Exploring ourselves through meditation, we open up to noticing the whole organism, not just selected bits. In this sense certainly, meditation is integrative *inwardly*; however, it is also integrative *outwardly*.

I was once chatting with a fellow attorney at the end of a closing while we were waiting for the money transfer. He knew that I practiced meditation and asked what it was about, so I gave him the elevator speech about sitting and noticing thoughts and how numerous they are. The next day he phoned me and said that his drive home after our talk had been one of the scariest experiences he'd ever had: "I realized that most of the time I wasn't paying any attention to where I was going. I was on autopilot!"

The sense of being *outwardly integrative*—noticing how your mind interacts with the world you inhabit—means that instead of picking and choosing what we prefer to attend to in the ongoing flux of phenomena that makes up life, we engage with openness whatever arises. We can be in this world as well as of it, an integral presence with allegiance to the reality we inhabit.

We can do this because what you experience through meditation is always available, not just when you are formally engaged in meditation practice. The sense of presence, the mind that you make friends with in meditation is the same one through which you engage with the rest of your life. Meditation is not a hobby to do in your spare time or after you retire from your life's work but is relevant at every stage of life. The spillover from recognizing your tendency to be distracted by thoughts in meditation practice means you can't help noticing how that happens when you are talking to a co-worker or family member.

These *integrative* aspects are reflected in the meditation technique. Sometimes people find it surprising that this meditation practice is done with the eyes open and ask, "But isn't it easier to relax, to chill out, with my eyes closed?" The answer to that question is that it might be, but the point of this kind of meditation isn't to help us relax and chill out. It is to help wake us up, to bring us into the present moment, into simple presence. Once we realize that we can be present in any situation, the ability to be relaxed (which can include what people think of as managing stress) in any situation naturally comes along; however, it is more of a side effect than a primary objective.

Learning by Doing

In addition to being integrative, mindfulness is *empirical.* Meditation practitioners learn through experience, witnessing first-hand how thoughts and emotions arise and then go away. In a sense, you could say that you are introducing yourself to the obvious, to experiences that are right there for you to see—a perspective you hadn't noticed before. There is no need to adopt a belief system which, in any case, could be right, wrong, or beside the point.

Learning in this way, your mind becomes something you can recognize, just like any part of your experience: the neighborhood grocery store, or the place where you live. Because the experience of spacing out into the distraction of thoughts has become vividly apparent in meditation, you also know and recognize it when you are doing routine tasks, like driving a car or talking to a friend. Learning to separate mental chatter from reality comes naturally. No one needs to tell you that it is happening, just like no one needs to tell you when you arrive in front of your house. You simply know it.

And when you know it, you automatically and intuitively know what to do, which is to come back to being present. In fact, by the time you recognize that you have been distracted, you are already back in the present. You don't need to look it up or call an expert; you just know it. Once people are exposed to presence as a real experience, its value is obvious to them and they gravitate toward it naturally.

As this experience deepens, simply going about your ordinary business you notice over and over that moments of presence are occurring. And as they become more frequent and apparent, you begin to realize—from experience—that they are always available. Recognizing moments of presence in ordinary life situations can, like the sitting meditation practice, become a kind of practice; you learn from what you observe about your state of mind as you move through everyday life. As in the sitting practice, the fact that you are not always in the present is not a problem.

The crux of this learning experience is the contrast between habitual thinking and simple presence—that moment when you come back to your awareness of the present moment and notice sense perceptions. When you see that difference over and over in the meditation practice, it becomes a natural part of what you know, just like looking out the window and being able to tell whether it is day, night, or somewhere in between.

When first practicing in this way, you apply the deliberate technique of noticing the difference, in that you acknowledge the existence of the thinking process and then go back to being simply present with your sense perceptions and bodily sensations. As you become more experienced, you begin to get a feel for the difference between being caught up in thoughts or emotions and simply being present. You don't have to talk to yourself about it, but you recognize it from experience. Just as you don't need to tell yourself not to walk into a lamppost, you just do it. It is as if you have developed a knack for noticing the difference.

As this takes hold as a part of your everyday experience, you are better able to avoid the pitfalls that come with not having the proper "operating instructions" for your equipment. Your perception is clarified and heightened. You miss fewer things, and the subtleties of what you experience become more apparent. And as the thinking process becomes more transparent, it tends less and less to color or distort your perceptions. The knack for recognizing habitual patterns helps cool habitual reactivity and lets you simply experience what is happening, what is said, what gestures are made, the tone of voice of others—and even your own.

This is vividly different from our common experience of being so involved in habitual commentary that we literally don't see what's in front of us or hear ambient sounds, moments when we are temporarily deaf and blind. With enough practice, there is a shift of perception—the development of mindfulness muscles—that enables us to be present *and* think or speak without one blocking out the other; this is the gateway to applying mindfulness in everyday life.

The Momentum of Distraction

In meditation you learn to see the tendency of mind to translate the heat of emotions into a story that you tell yourself—and sometimes others—to rationalize your reaction to upsetting experiences. Everyone has had the experience of blurting out something in the heat of the moment and almost immediately being seized with regret. Through the practice of mindfulness, you begin to experience your emotions earlier, when they began just to cast their shadow before them. This renders them more like a well-predicted storm than an unforeseen disaster, offering you the opportunity to avoid being automatically swept away by a habitual reaction.

Just as we don't reject thoughts in meditation, we don't reject our emotions; nor do we, out of a misguided sense of genuineness or authenticity, have to justify or attempt to justify acting them out. "I was just being honest" is a classic rationalization, although honesty is not always the most skillful policy. Practicing mindfulness meditation, we can become familiar with our emotions and discover those to which we have a particular attraction.

The next step occurs when, rather than confusing the emotions with the story lines that reflexively seem to tag along, we begin to notice the feel or energy of the emotion itself. Then, of course, we can feel that energy and manage it wherever it occurs, whether sitting in meditation or engaged in a meeting, negotiation, or other interaction.

The combination of thoughts with this emotional energy is what gives distractions and habitual patterns a sense of momentum; they are not just static occurrences but have a feeling of movement. It is that movement or momentum that sometimes results in our saying or doing things that we later regret. The upside—so to speak—of the momentum is its vividness, which helps make the whole process more noticeable. In terms of applying mindfulness, the vivid momentum of the emotional/thinking process actually helps us see it better, so that we can relate with it mindfully instead of habitually.

If we can recognize the momentum without denying it out of embarrassment, then the recognition itself can simply act as a reminder to let go of the pattern and return to being present. In fact, as our perceptions are clarified through mindfulness meditation, we begin to recognize that it was a moment of presence itself that interrupted the momentum.

Building Mindfulness Muscles

I t may seem odd to talk about mindfulness muscles, but in some ways meditation is like any other form of exercise, building strength and endurance. People who work out regularly in gyms do so because they know that regular application of exercise is the only way to bring desired results. It is the same with meditation, and although you can't physically measure its results as you can with biceps or quads, you can feel the difference.

But just as toning physical muscles isn't limited to time at the gym, cultivating mindfulness muscles doesn't stop when our timer rings. You can also cultivate recognizing presence in everyday life situations. A method I used when my most of my days were spent in a law office involved answering the phone. Rather than immediately grabbing the receiver and starting to speak, I would put my hand on it and pause for a moment, resting in presence. Only then would I pick it up and say "hello". It's a highly effective way to cultivate presence in the midst of the momentum of work.

With regular meditation practice the experience of being present, becoming distracted, and noticing that becomes familiar, so that you notice the contrast more quickly, whether in formal practice or as you go about other parts of your life. You notice getting distracted when trying to listen to another person, or when you yourself are talking. You start to recognize the feel of high-momentum thoughts and begin learning how not to get ensnared. In short, while your physical muscles allow you to flex and hold, your mindfulness muscles allow you to relax, notice, and release into simple presence.

Develop them well enough and they will definitely give you an inner advantage.

PART TWO

2

Fear:
The Untapped Asset

Avoiding the Obvious

F ear, for an emotion that affects so many, is oddly ignored
in conversation. We are especially reticent about the personal experience of it. Of course, it does get a fair amount of
play in politics, where fear of loss is a strong motivator, and
vivid pathological examples of it sometimes make the news,
as when hoarders cut themselves off from human interaction
altogether. But it often seems hard to acknowledge that we
have fear, much less to talk about our relationship with it.

But all people experience fear, and in all walks of life, including at work and at home. It's a common experience and
not at all aberrant. Broaching the issue in mindfulness trainings for professional people—and these are not reclusive
folks— I've never heard anybody say that they never feel fear;
they just don't see much point in talking about it. That
changes when I suggest that fear can be an ally.

Instead of feeling like weakness to be hidden, fear can be
turned it into a source of strength by approaching it with
mindfulness. If that sounds questionable, it's because of the
ambivalent attitude most of us have toward fear. We're both
attracted and repelled; we watch scary movies but sometimes
avert our eyes. From minor nervousness to heart-pounding
panic, whether triggered by something as big as a potentially
mortal medical diagnosis or something as small as being startled when the phone rings, fear is something we generally
prefer not to feel.

Thus we miss many chances to tap into the energy of
fear and harness it. Because regardless of where on the hierarchy of fears any particular episode may lie—from true
terror to trivial annoyance—it has a common feeling. And
so, in the practices this book suggests, we treat all instances
of fear the same: we learn to recognize the feeling common
throughout the spectrum, which we'll call the fear-feeling,

and to distinguish that feeling from the story that follows in its wake. Then, applying mindfulness, we can boycott the tales we tell ourselves about fear and instead ride the energy of the feeling, staying present and curious about what is there.

Questions about fear as a survival instinct are sometimes raised in meditation training classes, but rather than examining fear's origins, in this book we simply will take it as a fact of life to be explored using mindfulness. This approach opens our potential to be effective human beings because we can use the energy of fear to as a springboard to greater presence and engagement.

To begin, we need to acknowledge our almost reflexive desire to avoid fear. Even if we believe intellectually that fear has survival value, when it raises its vivid head we often want no part of it. In a book called *The Gift of Fear*, Gavin de Becker, a security consultant, vividly illustrates this in numerous stories about how otherwise intelligent individuals ignored fear signals, sometimes to their fatal detriment. In one example, he describes a group in a business debating whether a suspiciously wrapped package might be from the Unabomber and eventually deciding their concerns were irrational paranoia. The box exploded when they opened it.

De Becker points out how people often ignore the fear that they experience. We've all heard stories like this: someone has an initial cautious feeling about a situation which is discounted, thinking, "Oh, this nice person's offering to help me with the bags that I'm taking out to my car in the parking lot. I'm so silly to be afraid when they must just be trying to be helpful." Well, sometimes they are, but sometimes they're not. Applying mindfulness to fear can help us tell the difference.

When we apply mindfulness, we can test the hypothesis that we engage in habitual mental and behavioral patterns as an avoidance strategy when the feeling of fear arises. Attending to these patterns, we can also explore whether the feeling of fear might be arising more frequently than we consciously acknowledge.

I use the word "hypothesis" deliberately; this is something to explore in your own experience as an exercise in mindfulness, an approach to fear that will only have meaning for you if you confirm it in your own experience. Adopting a theory as a belief is not enough because it tends to put an end to inquiry; however, treating the idea that habitual patterns may be generated as a smokescreen to cover fear is a hypothesis you can explore. Nervousness, anxiety, the sudden desire to be very busy: all these experiences and more can be examined with mindfulness, and what you discover can be applied to situations you encounter every day.

Fear and Its Uses

From the viewpoint of those who try to manipulate the attitudes and behaviors of others, fear is a valued tool. For example, if you contemplate the behavior of organizations seeking funding, politicians seeking votes, or bosses enforcing compliance, you may notice occasions when they deliberately cultivate fear, often suggesting that the resolution lies in reliance on the purveyor of the fear to deal with the problem. Hence, fear can be cultivated for self-serving purposes.

On a closer-to-home level, in relationships between individuals, fear can be invoked in a message of intimidation, as in emotional blackmail. Of course, extortionists and blackmailers use it as a technique for doing business, but even on a level that does not involve criminality, fear can be invoked for leverage: "If you don't do what I want you to do then I will make your life unpleasant in some way"—fire you, divorce you, exclude you from my social circle, or whatever the particular context may be.

De Becker's book, which calls fear a gift, brings helpful balance to the topic. He doesn't suggest being fearful all the time, because that—living with the attitude that you've always got to be on the lookout—distorts your perceptions; you see everything through a filter of fearfulness. But learning how, through mindfulness meditation, to let go of constant mental commentary means that, when fear actually arises, you may recognize it as such.

Then you can see if it holds a message. You can look to see what its source is, without lapsing into a habitual story line. You can feel its energy in your body. You can be curious about it. This approach allows you to make fear a positive factor in how you live your life, rather than tuning into it solely to try to avoid harm to person or property. It may sound counterintuitive, but fear can deepen your ability to stay present.

The Spectrum of Fear

Until we learn how to stay with fear mindfully and consciously, the tendency to avoid feeling it has the upper hand. We spin off into mental chatter, concepts, explanations, excuses, and opinions, rather than simply experiencing the fear for what it is. Although when we think of fear in the abstract, we may focus on dire situations (such as being mugged, environmental catastrophe, or terrorism), it's more helpful to look for it in ordinary life situations.

That's because ordinary life is where we find fear's diversions usually arising. If fear occurred only in situations of extreme peril, it would be harder to cultivate a healthy response, but everyday situations provide an abundance of opportunities for experiencing the fear feeling and allowing us to become familiar with how to make fear one of our assets.

The first step is to recognize the feeling. It's easy to feel fear when a car is careening toward us, or we get a phone call in the middle of the night; fear of threats and tangible misfortune is likewise fairly obvious. But we also fear lots of things that we may never have identified as triggering fear, things like space and ambiguity.

Consider the fear of boredom. We may not even think of it as fear but how many of us feel unsettled when there is nothing going on to grasp our attention? We're not quite sure what to do with that unsettled feeling and our reflexive reaction is often to fill up the "empty" space with something. It could be obsessing, turning on the TV, exploring the fridge, or cleaning our house—anything to avoid just being in a space where nothing's going on.

People fear the inevitable uncertainty that's part of life. We may feel uncertain about the future, trying to plan for desired results, and about the past, trying to understand (and perhaps excuse) things that have already happened. In either case, uncertainty almost always generates fear, and in response to fear, we react. One reaction to fear about the future is to attempt to manipulate the variables (or as many as we can) so things work out the way we want and we can feel as if we're in control. This sometimes works but when it fails it can feel catastrophic. As for uncertainty about the past, our reaction is usually to conjure a coherent story that either justifies our behavior or pre-empts criticism by taking pro-active blame. Either way, we create a story to help mask the fear feeling.

Fear of rejection may entice us to avoid situations where that might happen. If we fear being rejected by our boss, we may engage in flattery or sucking up behavior, hoping to be liked. Or we may avoid commitment to a relationship, a job, or a friendship, believing that if we don't commit, nobody can reject us.

More generally, it may be that we fear disappointment of any sort. So we might avoid making plans altogether. Or we might be quick when our plans don't work out to blame other people or make excuses, seeing ourselves as victimized by the situation. "I never really had a chance, you know, because so-and-so had the edge on me there and so-and-so likes him better."

Perhaps the ultimate fear we have is of death, which is yet another variety of uncertainty—at least as to the when, as we human beings have a mortality rate of precisely 100 percent. We hope that if we eat the right food, if we run enough, if we do enough exercise, we'll somehow fend that off—or at least delay it—and we often apply such strategies without even being aware that they have anything to do with fear.

That's because these strategies can all be used as forms of avoidance. When we find ourselves being speedy, blaming other people, denying the existence of some situation, or engaging in any activity to mask the experience of fear, we are trying to avoid reality: fear is actually present in our experience and we don't know how to work with it. We have never learned that is it not only possible, but actually energizing, to simply be present with fear.

A few years back I got a medical diagnosis that could have triggered one of these responses. After PSA test results prompted a biopsy, I was diagnosed with early stage prostate cancer. Having a potentially mortal condition was a totally new experience for me, although one I would repeat, and double down on, within a few years. So I have personal experience of how challenging it is when the experience of fear arises in a situation with such high stakes. And I know how fortunate I am to have learned a way to tap the assets within everything from the tiniest twinges to the most massive and relentless waves of fear.

Avoidance and Habitual Patterns

To avoid experiencing the gritty quality of fear, we generate habitual patterns of thought and activity, often busying ourselves with something besides the fear, either inwardly, outwardly, or with some combination of the two. Inwardly, our minds may generate repetitive patterns. For example, when afraid, people sometimes engage in internal conversations which attempt to explain or justify their attitudes or actions. Or their mental contents may incline them to finding fault with the attitudes and actions of others.

Outwardly, constant activity can be an avoidance behavior. From the moment of waking up in the morning until going to bed at night, we try to make sure that there is always something going on. Work may provide yeoman service for a good part of the day, but that still leaves a few hours when we are at loose ends. In those situations we seek out other activities to occupy our time. Some of these may be active, such as an exercise regime or a hobby, while others are more passive, such as watching television or reading a magazine.

Some patterns link our inner and outer habits. For example, in relations with other people, we may habitually fill up the space with talk, regardless of whether or not the talk is relevant to the interaction. This is an outer analog to filling one's mind with thoughts. At the other end of the spectrum, we may clam up, protecting ourselves from criticism by not expressing anything with which anyone might find fault.

There is nothing inherently wrong with any of these activities—working, exercising, reading, talking, or being silent—any one of them can be engaged in while in a state of presence. The challenge is to recognize when you are in the grip of a habitual pattern so that you can let it go and return to whatever is right in front of you.

Avoidance and Deception

When you try to avoid the experience of fear, you divide your awareness between direct experience and the avoidance behavior. As you come to see this more clearly, you may realize that the avoidance behavior often results in expressing yourself disingenuously; you're trying to convince yourself and the people around you that things—whether situations in the material world or your state of mind—are a certain way. This avoidance dynamic is a prime suspect in the deceptiveness discussed in Part One of this book in the section on mindful living.

Observing your interactions with others mindfully, you see how you sometimes try to create an impression or put a "spin" on a situation. On occasion you may notice that you are not only attempting to influence others (not necessarily a bad thing) but also trying to convince yourself of your compelling interpretation. If you value personal integrity, it's difficult to convince somebody else of something you're not convinced of yourself; however, if you first convince yourself, then that issue disappears. Convincing ourselves of something that's advantageous even if not objectively credible is a common habitual trap.

Except where only clearly quantifiable matters are involved, any description of a situation is inevitably abstracted from the fullness of the experience itself. Trying to describe a color or a taste demonstrates easily how words fall short; describing the intentions of others or the likely outcome of a strategy is even more difficult. When you have a vested interest in the outcome, the stakes are raised, and spinning a situation to your advantage can be a temptation.

Approaching such situations mindfully and with integrity, you have an opportunity to develop clarity. You can acknowledge that the underlying assumptions may not reflect the whole story, not because the particular assumptions are faulty, but because it's in the nature of assumptions to be incomplete. Recognizing the possible influence of habitual patterns in shaping those assumptions may expose weaknesses that you overlooked when your objective was focused solely on convincing others.

Calling these activities deceptive may, at first, seem too strong. Sometimes it may simply be a matter of misapprehension or error. However, staying on the lookout for self-deception may keep us from missteps we may later regret.

The Fear and the Story

Because of fear's potential to be a valuable asset in our lives, it's to our advantage to recognize it. The challenge is similar to that in recognizing presence—the experience of presence is, in the untrained mind, so thoroughly intertwined with the accompanying commentary that it's hard to tell them apart. This is why, in the practice of meditation, noticing the difference between simply being present and being occupied with thoughts is emphasized. Because the experience of presence is so quiet, and the thinking process is so content-ridden, it can take a while for the contrast to become clear and the gaps of presence to be noticed.

Learning to work mindfully with fear poses a similar challenge. The jolt of the basic energy or feeling of fear is so quickly accompanied by a story line that the story line itself captures our attention, and the direct experience of fear can be ignored. Paralleling the meditation experience of noticing glimpses of presence until it's more obvious to you, working with fear requires a similar awareness; but in this case, it is attuned to the experience of fear itself.

To work with fear this way requires learning to recognize and then appreciate the feeling of it. Although most people conceptualize fear as a mental or emotional experience, the feeling of fear is actually bodily. It can be a tingle of energy up the spine, a sensation of heaviness or density in the chest or abdomen, or even nausea. Individual experiences vary, but once the feeling becomes familiar, you can, as with presence, become attuned to it so that you can stay present without being swept up in the story that inevitably accompanies it.

Thus you can discriminate between the feeling of fear and the story line about the fear. Like recognizing thoughts, recognizing the story line—a combination of thought and emotion—can become a knack, something that becomes a mindfulness muscle. Naturally, because generating story lines is an old pattern, many times you will find yourself immersed in the story, having missed the initial feeling of fear.

When that happens, you may be able to backtrack and recall the first flash of fear that you covered up with the story. Or the simple recognition that you're caught in a story may remind you instantaneously of the moment of fear that triggered it. Or something may dawn much later in a similar experience after you have become better sensitized to recognizing the fear feeling. If you are like most people, persistence in applying mindfulness in various ways will be needed to clarify your experience of the feeling of fear.

Recognizing the Energy of Fear

C larifying the feeling of fear allows us to begin to harness its energy. The basic tool, mindfulness meditation, enhances your sensitivity to events that occur in your mind, and so becomes a way to approach the many elements of the mind, including fear. Naturally, it is possible to recognize fear—and possibly to distinguish it from the accompanying story line—without practicing meditation; however, meditation makes the experience more readily apparent.

Fears involving personal safety or survival are generally too sporadic to provide a working basis for learning to tap into fear. Also, not every experience of fear is shockingly intense; the fear feeling can be subtle, such as when we're waiting for an important phone call; however, if you cultivate your perception through meditation practice, your ability to recognize the subtleties increases.

Acquainting yourself with fear, you recognize that the experience is composed of several parts—thoughts, feelings, and bodily sensations. By the time we identify fear arising, it is almost always accompanied by thoughts relating to its origin, who's to blame, how to get rid of it, and so forth. The thoughts are colored by a feeling with emotional content. Fear is also felt as a bodily sensation, as described earlier. However you encounter fear, recognizing the parts is essential to working with it mindfully.

Although the fear feeling may arise during formal meditation sessions, much of this exploration takes place in ordinary life situations, post-meditation. You don't need to seek out frightening situations or become an adrenalin junkie; once sensitized to the experience, you can recognize it easily and notice that it happens frequently—you don't have to try to conjure it up. As my south Georgia grandmother was fond of saying, "Sufficient unto the day is the evil thereof." Or as we might say in the current argot, don't go looking for trouble.

Instead, you can cultivate your recognition of the fear feeling by working with trivial things to which you might not otherwise give a second thought. You may be startled by the ringing of the telephone or the slamming of a door. You might feel nervous before giving a speech, approaching an investor, meeting with a client, or asking for a raise. Asking for help in the workplace is another common source of fear or nervousness because of uncertainty about the outcome.

When situations like these bring fear up, you will only recognize it if you know what it feels like. That initial experience of the fear feeling, which is what you're trying to notice, is the basis for cultivating presence and ultimately a heightened sense of confidence. While FDR may have oversimplified things in saying "the only thing we have to fear is fear itself," it is true that if we are not afraid of fear, we will find it easier to stay present and confident.

Some entertain the notion, consciously or unconsciously, that experiencing and acknowledging fear is a sign of weakness; however, numerous accounts of courage on the battlefield belie that. Courageous action, even at the risk of one's life, is not a matter of being without fear but of being willing to act anyway.

How to Work with Fear

The first step in working with fear is learning that it is not an obstacle to accomplishing your objectives; instead obstacles are more likely to arise in the attempt to avoid or buffer the feeling of fear. Whether you find yourself freezing up, talking too much, or saying things you don't believe because you feel they'll be acceptable to your listeners, you are engaging in avoidance tactics that make it harder to meet the moments of your life directly.

If you try to dodge fear in moment-to-moment situations often enough, avoidance of fear becomes a lifestyle. It can make you less adventurous so that you won't take chances, even if they might open up new opportunities. Because new opportunities bring new challenges, you may say "No, thanks," or you may simply shun situations that might pull you out of your comfort zone.

Avoidance became ingrained in our psyches as a strategic response from an early age, where the fear feeling arose and we were gripped in the impulse of fight, flight, or freeze. Whether we fumbled a football, forgot lines in a play or notes in a piece of music, or didn't know the answer when called on, we felt the discomfort of embarrassment. Or the pain of loss or the sting of rejection made us feel bad.

Whatever the situations might have been, we were afraid they would happen again. Since we didn't have a way of working with the experience of fear directly, we began to strategize how to avoid such situations altogether. In other words, we became afraid of experiencing fear and as a result tried to steer clear of situations that might trigger it. But it doesn't have to be that way.

Working with fear directly in "real life" situations involves three steps:

1. The first is to *recognize*, in the midst of a situation, the feeling of fear. If you explore enough small situations of fear, the feeling becomes familiar. Having recognized how fear feels, you can deliberately pay attention to it so that even when you slide off into habitual patterns and story lines, your awareness of the fear feeling gets closer to the surface and more available. (Don't worry about slip-ups; they're just part of the process.) Experiencing fear without lapsing into habitual patterns invokes presence. Although this may initially seem counterintuitive, connecting with fear in this way, just like connecting with the feeling of any emotional experience without drifting into the story line, brings us into the present moment so that mindfulness is possible.

2. The second step is to *stay with the fear*. Stay present with it, and don't turn away into habitual patterns. Don't be afraid that if you don't get rid of it, fear will last forever. Fear, like all feelings, eventually passes.

Conversely, you don't need to perpetuate the fear to stay with it. Just experience it for as long as it lasts. Notice this, for example, when you're waiting for an important meeting; when you feel the fear, just stay with it, and don't try to mask it by distracting yourself until the meeting begins.

3, The third step: having recognized and stayed with the fear feeling, simply *proceed with whatever it is you're doing*. As in the phone call example, after resting in the fear feeling, answer the phone, and engage with the conversation. Transitioning to this step is in some ways the most challenging part. Experiencing fear directly in this way can make you feel vulnerable and exposed; it takes genuine effort to stay with it at first, but with practice, it becomes accessible.

In summary, here are the fear practice's three steps:

✧ *Feel the fear;*
✧ *Stay with it, not lapsing into avoidance behaviors;*
✧ *Proceed with what you're doing.*

The process sounds simple, and on an intellectual level it is; however, actually applying it in everyday life requires going beyond merely knowing the steps. The heart of the practice is learning to trust that if you allow yourself to remain in simple presence, your intelligence will still be available to you, engaging with the situation effectively. The challenge is that letting go into the space of presence involves losing a sense of control. Even when you recognize that the sense of control is illusory, or at best partial, letting go of it can be a fearful experience.

When I was engaged in the full-time practice of law working with clients structuring transactions, I noticed a habit I had. Rather than simply taking notes as the client described

the deal, I was often simultaneously planning the legal structure, the documents that would be needed, the time frame
we were working with, the team I would need to assemble,
and any legal issues requiring research. It was all very reassuring, giving me the sense that I knew what I was doing,
that I had a grip.

What was not so satisfying was that often, well into the
description of the business transaction, my client would mention something that didn't fit the plan I was already construct-
ing. It was like I'd been building a house with a standard
plan, only to suddenly realize that I had to add a wing I hadn't
taken into account before.

Recognizing the incongruity between what I was doing
at work and what I was teaching in meditation classes—to
trust that intelligence would arise from presence—I resolved
that, at the next opportunity, I would put off the legal planning until I had heard everything my client had to say. I had
previously used this approach to meeting fear in a number
of other situations, but taking it into my law practice was a
new step.

It wasn't easy—the first time doing things often isn't—but
I figuratively gritted my teeth and started taking notes of what
the client was telling me. It was a revelation. After I'd heard
the details of the transaction, my transactional lawyer training
automatically kicked in, and the legal structuring of the transaction arose very easily. Unlike the results of my previous approach, the resulting structure was elegant; there was no
awkward additional wing on the house that I had to deal with.

What a relief. The next time a situation like this arose, it
was much easier. I'd actually developed genuine confidence that
I could do what was needed without relying upon an illusory
feeling of being in control. I also realized that the entire process
had become considerably more relaxed because I didn't constantly have to divide my attention between listening and plan-

ning. The experience of presence was manifesting vividly in a law office. Who would have thought such a thing possible?

When you first let go of control, it's a revelation to realize that things won't blow up in your face simply because you experience fear. Fear doesn't have to be a devastating experience, nor need it make you dysfunctional. You begin to appreciate that you can stay with fear and still respond intelligently; further confidence arises from that. You realize that your relationship to your world is not transitory, that the connection with it need not be disrupted simply because you experience fear.

As a result, the bugaboo of fear turns out to be a gift that helps you wake up to presence because you can engage with your experience so directly. If you try to stay insulated so that you never experience fear, then you will always have a gray, mushy relationship to your world, filtered through your avoidance strategies. But if you stay with the fear feeling, you can see the sharpness of your experience when it arises, be present with it, and be who you are.

So I have come to rely on the fear feeling whenever I go into challenging situations, such as leading a workshop, or making a speech, or having an initial meeting with a client. I even become a bit suspicious if I don't have that feeling, wondering if I'm unconsciously relying on some habitual pattern rather than being present in the situation. Thus, working with fear in this way, it can become a cue.

Going into a meeting where you have something at stake is an example. Perhaps your department's budget is being reviewed. Or you are receiving the results of an annual performance evaluation. Conversely, you may be presenting the results of an evaluation to someone in your department. In any of those situations you can come to find the feeling of fear or nervousness to be reassuring—odd as that may sound. It is a clear message that your human equipment and its sensory devices are actually working as they're supposed to do.

Rousing Energy: Fear's Hidden Bonus

D emanding situations that do not have clear resolutions naturally generate more energy around them than do routine ones. Whether you call it "fear" or "excitement" is really a matter of attitude. So far we've mostly addressed how to reach a state of peaceful coexistence with fear. Realizing that the difficulties we previously thought of as products of fear are actually based on our avoidance of it, we can appreciate that it's possible to function perfectly well even in the presence of fear, further confirming that presence is available whenever we remember to notice.

As calming as it is to drop habitual ways of relating to fear and simply be present with it, there is even more to be gained by connecting with a dimension of fear that is energizing. Of course it takes a while to fully engage with this on an experiential level. It's not enough simply to think, "Fear is energizing." Cultivating that belief may be a beneficial temporary expedient, but ultimately the energizing quality is something you need to feel with your whole being, including the physical sensations. You can access this through cultivating presence.

As the experience of the fear feeling becomes more familiar, you realize that you can harness its energy, like a trusty steed. The energy associated with fear actually perks you up and helps you to connect with whatever situation you're in. Often this is as simple as being willing to pause and look around you, to feel out the situation you are in, to know who it is you are talking to. Then when you speak or act, you can do so without being bullied by unreliable habitual patterns. The heaviness of the habitual patterns will no longer weigh you down, and you can function with lightness and humor, even in difficult and challenging situations.

Through repeated exposure to the presence of fear, you can appreciate how fickle and unreliable your habitual attempts to manage it were. Recognizing fear becomes a durable source of confidence. When we rely on habit to control fear, what works one time fails another. On the other hand, when we welcome fear it becomes a reliable companion. We are familiar with the feel of it and understand that we don't have to run away.

Problem-laden situations beget fear. But why do we see problems as "problems"? One reason is that they often contain facts we didn't expect to have to deal with, and for which, as a result, we have no plan of action, a classic trigger for uncertainty. Seeing uncertainty as a normal part of life will help you to appreciate that not immediately having a "solution" for the uncertainty is also part of the norm.

Recognizing the absence of a ready solution and being willing to stay with that rather than scrambling to fill the space (an avoidance response) is what Michael Carroll calls "the wisdom of not knowing" in *Fearless at Work*. Resting in not knowing provides a fertile ground for insights to occur.

People are also uncomfortable with problems because they can interfere with desired outcomes. Frustration of hopes creates a further situation of uncertainty (what happens now that the plan didn't pan out?), and can sometimes flip us reflexively into a habitual reaction, such as blaming someone else or yourself. In these situations it's helpful to remember that there's a difference between actual frustration (the fact that things didn't work out as planned) and *feeling* frustrated (an emotion you add reactively). The latter doesn't help, so just let it go. It's often accompanied by thoughts, which make it more easily recognizable.

If you can relax with uncertainty because you have learned to coexist with the energy of the fear feeling, then you can remain open without filling the space with aspersions or harried attempts to produce a solution. For problems without an easy solution, the ability to hang out in that space of not knowing is a productive way to allow potential solutions to occur to you. That space allows creativity and insight to occur; neither can be pushed.

It is also possible to use the wisdom of uncertainty deliberately. I used to be a part of the leadership group in a nonprofit organization that used "brainstorming" as one of the techniques for planning. Brainstorming involves generating ideas for later consideration, with the ground rule that none of the ideas are critiqued or analyzed when spoken. Although people in brainstorming sessions usually suggest ideas they favor, during one of these sessions an idea occurred to me that I hadn't considered before, so in the spirit of brainstorming, I blurted it out. Afterward, when we had moved into the discussion session, someone made reference to the idea that I had "advocated." I hadn't actually thought the idea through—it had just come up—so I was not advocating the idea but just tossing it out. It was actually fine with me if the idea turned out to be a loser, but we'd never find out unless it was on the table. It's an example of something I have learned to value—being willing to be wrong, a corollary of the wisdom of not knowing.

Previously, a three-step strategy to working with fear was described. Of course, there are others. For example, at a recent leadership training one of the participants described a fear-elimination strategy. "I've noticed that when I'm feeling nervous or afraid, if I think, what is the worst thing that can happen? the fear often just dissipates, and I can go on without having to deal with it." The technique she was describing, sometimes called "inoculation," was championed by another group member as well.

I suspect that inoculation does work in a lot of situations to dissipate the experience of fear, but it's at the cost of losing the potential for being energized by fear. Just as it is an erroneous notion that thoughts are something to be gotten rid of in meditation, it's also an erroneous notion that fear is something to rid yourself of in life situations. Fear avoidance strategies actually buy into the idea that fear creates obstacles, whereas the approach of this book is that it is the avoidance of fear—by lapsing into habitual patterns such as fight, flight, or freeze—that gets in the way.

Of course, while you're getting used to the approach suggested here, it may be helpful to use inoculation or other techniques; but eventually you can wean yourself from them.

Dynamic Equanimity

When you combine presence with the determination to stay with fear, you avail yourself of a state that can be called "dynamic equanimity," the ability to remain present in the midst of activity. Inevitably you'll encounter situations that are difficult and challenging, and they will occur not only in situations that are "problems." Positive developments can also have difficulties, such as when a customer or client places a huge order or initiates a large process or case that you'll have to stretch to meet. Dynamic equanimity allows you to cut through the resulting anxiety and agitation and meet the situation with mindfulness, staying present without panicking and ultimately giving you a greater chance of success.

Dynamic equanimity doesn't guarantee coming up with a perfect answer, strategy, or response; rather, it means that you can bring the focus that you discover through sitting meditation into the midst of activity or action. It's not a matter of becoming even or smooth but of becoming a resourceful person.

Often when people talk about human nature, it's with a wistful quality tinged with regret, as if making allowances for unfortunate behavior. "That's just human nature!" However, it's interesting to consider what mindfulness reveals about "human nature." For one, we are all different. No two of us have the same experiences. At the same time the *way* we function as human beings shares common characteristics. We have in common how experience arises: we all have thoughts and emotions, and we all have the ability to connect with simple presence. Because of the shared basis of experience, insights about it can be expressed to others and applied by them.

Mindfulness meditation leads you to understand that you can accommodate your thoughts, whatever they may be and however they may depart from a carefully groomed self-image. Having "disturbing" thoughts or emotions doesn't have to disturb you. They're just thoughts and emotions; they come and they go, but they aren't fixed, immutable parts of who you are. If you take note of your emotions and how they feel, the familiarization process allows them to inform future behaviors and generate further confidence.

Confidence arises because when you learn to recognize and stay with the fear feeling, you realize that you can accommodate any situation. Just because you feel fear in a situation doesn't mean that you have to avoid it. Instead, the confidence cultivated through fearlessly relating to fear leads to a genuine attitude of humility. This is not humility in the sense of "Oh, poor me, I don't know what to do," but rather a willingness to remain open, to see what you can learn from observing the situation, your responses to it, and the responses of others.

As confidence builds, you'll realize that you can stay with your experience more and more, and when you do, your awareness naturally expands, bringing you into closer connection with the events of your life. Whereas the mechanism of generating thoughts, concepts, and opinions tends to insulate you from your experience, if you can avoid getting stuck in them, your awareness naturally goes outward. It is a very simple and ordinary occurrence.

Think about presence or awareness like vision: if you open your eyes, you see what's in front of you. You don't have to try to make that happen, it just happens. And that's true of all of your senses. Your sense of presence is no different. There is an expansiveness that happens when you let go of your preoccupations with concepts and opinions about what's going on and rest in presence.

When you live with confidence, expansiveness and natural inquisitiveness arise. When you open your eyes and ears—if you're not caught up in thinking about what you see—you find your attention engaged by the world. It is a completely natural process and always available, if only you remember to notice. Having cultivated your awareness of how fears, thoughts, and emotions arise in your mind, you begin to trust that you can engage the world in the state of presence. You also find that often when you are caught up in your habitual patterns, the world—whether as a voice, an impressive vista, or a succulent aroma or taste—suddenly interrupts them, bringing you back into the present. Responding to your world in this way differs from habitual emotional reactivity; it is grounded in the experience of being present.

Meditation practice is a key technique for cultivating the clarity that makes mindful responsiveness possible. Thus meditation is not an end in itself but wakes you up to how your mind—your thoughts, emotions, feelings, and perceptions—actually works. That discovery allows you to experience whatever you encounter more fully and notice how you respond.

People sometimes labor under the misconception that if they just meditate enough, difficult emotions will stop arising, that somehow everything will be cooled out. In fact, once you open mindfully to the world and see, hear, and experience things without the habitual soundtrack, you still respond to them; your perceptions are not just images on a silent screen but will have a tone or feel to them. Situations, things, and people will continue to amuse or irritate, attract, or repel you. The difference is that you will have discovered how to avoid escalating the response into a story line or something you have to act on.

Whether you are responding to situations, objects, or other people, you always have a choice. You can use your response as a basis for stirring up familiar mental patterns, or you can notice the responsiveness, to see how it feels. Then, as with fear, you use it as a cue or reminder that you can simply be here, be present. Also, as with fear, you don't have to try to keep those responses from happening; let them happen, but don't hang onto them and generate lots of thoughts and opinions about them. A response happens, you notice it, and you let it go. And there you are, present again.

However, letting the response go doesn't mean that you ignore it. Instead, consider it as further information to take into account in guiding your activities going forward; rather than adopting the response as valid.

Relating to situations in this way brings genuine equanimity to your experience. You connect completely with whatever occurs and what it brings up in you. It is not a matter of smoothing things over—you can just be there with it. You don't have to get angry or upset about it, nor do you have to trumpet your response or solidify your point of view with it. Presence allows you to stay completely connected to whatever your experience is.

You benefit from acknowledging your responses, particularly when you have a queasy feeling about something that everybody else seems to be going along with or, conversely, when you have a positive feeling about something others are dismissing. Such situations definitely provide something further for you to examine, and you can look into whether avoiding the feeling of fear is getting in the way of communicating your take on the situation. It's an expression of trust in yourself.

Moreover, dynamic equanimity begins to permeate your presence. It affects your appearance and demeanor. Others come to see you as trustworthy and reasonable because you're not trying to make a big deal out of what happens. You're genuine about it; you don't tell other people that you had a different response to it than you did; sometimes you may say nothing at all.

I occasionally encounter people who say that the "mindful" approach to a situation or issue involves adopting a particular attitude or activity. This is true especially when discussing political topics. In effect they're trying to hijack mindfulness, to co-opt it in support of a particular agenda or point of view. This is not the function of mindfulness presented in this book; rather, the objective is to open to as complete an understanding of a situation as possible.

With mindfulness you remain on your own; the practice won't tell you the answer or what to do. Its point is to take you beyond your biases and other habitual patterns so that your intelligence and wisdom become deeper and broader. As this occurs, you will begin to be able to bring mindfulness to the process of making decisions.

Having addressed presence and fear in general terms, let's look at how they can be engaged in specific activities.

Fear: Challenge and Opportunity

The ability to relate to the fear feeling directly is crucial to applying mindfulness in professional situations. Even if you recognize distraction, without awareness of fear and the ability to stay with it in the face of difficulties, remaining focused can be swept away in the heat of the moment, resulting in errors of judgment and missed opportunities. Conversely, recognizing and learning how to stay with fear in the midst of activity enhances your engagement with any situation and your ability to respond skillfully without losing your connection with presence.

PART THREE

3

Everyday
Applications

Here are the basics for applying mindfulness in any situation:

✧ *Learn to recognize the experience of undistracted presence and how it feels different from being caught up in thoughts and emotions.*

✧ *Learn to recognize the feeling of fear or nervousness and distinguish it from the story lines generated around it.*

✧ *Learn to step into situations without relying on habitual patterns to buffer the fear feeling.*

✧ *Learn to enjoy the challenges life presents.*

Exploring situations that commonly occur in professional life and addressing the mindfulness issues arising in them—especially those involving the uncertainty/fear complex and the difficulties created by distraction or emotional reactivity—is the focus of this section. However, it's not just a problem-oriented exercise; we also explore how applying mindfulness can enhance skillful engagement in your world.

We'll look at the following categories: mindful decision-making, communication, creativity, and leadership.

Mindful Decision-Making

Because making decisions is an inescapable part of professional life, it is a fertile arena for examining the details of how you actually apply mindfulness. Choosing among options generally means addressing uncertainty; if all outcomes are obvious, the decision is already practically made. Moreover, since uncertainty often occasions nervousness and fear, situations in which we must make a decision offer the opportunity to observe how we deal with fear.

Mindfulness is the antidote to being distracted from presence. Since distraction results in missing or misinterpreting things rather than simply seeing them as they are, it adversely affects decision-making. Mindfulness can help us avoid responding to the wrong situation or the wrong question, or making a decision based on biased or distorted assumptions.

There is a different form of distraction that can also affect the decision-making process: the experience of speediness, of going too fast. The belief that there's a need for speed creates a sense of pressure to hurry up and make a decision, to get it done. Of course, sometimes decisions do have to be made quickly, but that's not always the case. In fact, some decisions, such as strategic planning, necessarily take place over an extended period. At other times, as when negotiating a deal with a third party, the timeline will depend on deadlines set by others; sometimes these deadlines are real, sometimes tactical, and sometimes ego-driven. Or a situation may seem urgent simply because we have a lot to do. Mindfulness provides a basis for discriminating between clear perceptions and habitual reactions.

In particular, a mindfulness technique called "contemplation" can be helpful. Contemplation, as we use the term here, is the practice of deliberately opening to insights or perspectives that might not yet have occurred to you. It can be done in five or ten minutes; you can take longer if you can spare the time. It's particularly helpful in making decisions when there's not an obvious answer or there's a judgment call among alternatives. (Appendix 3 provides a summary of contemplation for you to refer to as you become familiar with it.)

The contemplation technique is simple. The starting point is reconnecting with a sense of presence by sitting down in a quiet place and just being present. Then bring to mind the question or issue you want to address; it can be the pros and cons of a particular decision, the risk factors, your role in the decision, or any other question that has arisen. Know what your issue is but don't spend time trying to figure it out analytically; you've probably tried to do that already. Just hold the question as you rest in presence. Think of this period as simply letting the question "float," and see what arises.

One of the hardest parts of contemplation practice is deliberately not trying to figure out an answer. Here the "wisdom of not knowing" is the applicable slogan. Just create the open space for an insight to arise, knowing that it might or might not. Insights sometimes fail to arise simply because you want them so badly, a paradox I observed one day as I struggled contemplating a situation and got nowhere. Then, just as my timer dinged, an insight arose.

So instead of pressing for an answer, just rest in the space. Relax. If the fear feeling shows itself, let it energize your connection with presence.

These deceptively simple three steps can unleash powerful insight:

❖ Be *present*.
❖ Let the question *float*.
❖ Deliberately *avoid* trying to "figure out" the solution.

Moving on to the broader topic of how mindfulness can help us make decisions, let's address five aspects that illustrate its role in the process:

❖ preparation
❖ diverse perspectives
❖ risk assessment
❖ timing
❖ communicating the decision

Preparation

While it may seem obvious, we sometimes forget that the first step in preparation is to know just what it is we are preparing for so we don't jump the gun. Many of us learned this in school by writing the answer to a test without having finished reading the question. What a sinking feeling, to get the test back with, in addition to an inferior grade, a note from the teacher pointing out that if you'd read to the end you'd have known what question you were supposed to be answering. Taking in any situation fully before we react to it makes sense and cultivating mindfulness helps us slow down so we can do that. Speeding along with an assumption about what you're preparing for can waste a lot of time—or worse.

Preparation also involves being clear about your own role in the decision. That's not as simple as it sounds; understanding your role involves understanding the roles of others. Are you a first-year analyst gathering data for others to use? Are you a middle manager with responsibility for making a recommendation to the CEO or department head? Will the decision be made at an intermediate level, or will it go all the way to the top?

What if you are the first-year analyst and the CEO asks you if you agree with your superior's recommendation? Or if you are the middle manager, and the CEO asks if you believe that data backing up the decision are correct? Preparation helps you clarify elements you had anticipated and reveal those you had not; mindful preparation helps you expect the unexpected.

Being prepared for unexpected questions also requires broadening your view. For example, if you are employed by a manufacturing concern, do you have a clear understanding of your organization and how it is structured? Do you know how its products or services fit into the larger market, whether locally, regionally, nationally, or globally? Are you acquainted with the economic pressures in the nation or world at large, as well as the inevitable political uncertainties? Nobody can ever know how all these variables will play out, but you can know what they are and contemplate how certain of them might affect your decision.

Sometimes when asked to make a recommendation about a particular course of action, you may have an immediate gut feeling about it; however, preparing thoroughly means questioning that gut feeling as well. Instead of simply gathering data or evidence to support your first reaction, you have to explore the reasons that outcome might *not* work out well. Know a number of options, and their pros and cons. Expect that others involved in the decision-making process might have differing views, anticipate their concerns, and be prepared to defend your choice.

Having learned to recognize and rest in presence through mindfulness meditation, you can avoid the pitfalls that come from reacting too quickly. You will develop a knack for recognizing the "feel" of speeding along in habitual patterns and that feeling will cue you to simply pause for a moment to interrupt the momentum. Simultaneously, you may also recognize momentum as a reaction to fear that has arisen because of the pressurized situation. Letting the fear feeling reveal itself can energize your activity.

It can be helpful to use the contemplation method described above several times in the course of your preparation: perhaps at the start, midway through, and when approaching the end of the process, or as different issues arise.

Diverse Perspectives—Encouraging Critical Feedback

Mindfulness meditation teaches us to value a variety of perspectives. Seeing how unpredictable and fluid your own reactions to situations can be brings the insight that any single particular take on a situation—even your own—is partial at best. Through mindfulness practice, this understanding moves beyond the theoretical and becomes something that can be integrated into an approach to any situation.

Let's say that you've done your initial preparation for making a decision and that a possible approach has started to take shape. At that point, it's a good idea to ask people whom you trust to serve as your sounding board and offer a frank opinion on your prospective course.

At this point you need to be alert to the fear feeling. Asking for feedback involves uncertainty and, as a result, generally generates fear. When you ask others for help, fear finds fertile ground because you are making yourself vulnerable. People may say no because they don't have time, interest, or expertise. Or they may express willingness to help, but you realize in the course of the discussion that you really don't have their full attention, and you may be uncertain whether you actually have their commitment. Or they may disagree completely with your ideas and express that disagreement in unflattering terms. There's nothing that you can do to keep these things from happening—other than never asking for help, which is a pretty cowardly approach. Being willing to stick your neck out, using feedback situations, can help wake you up to the fear feeling, providing further familiarity with the feeling and enhancing your ability to harness that energy.

It's important not to miss the point when seeking feedback; this requires careful consideration of whom to ask for it. If you are just looking for confirmation and find a respondent who agrees with your conclusion, then you're done, mission accomplished. Or perhaps more cynically, you choose someone likely to agree because you're trying to hedge against a bad outcome and set the stage for deflecting blame by being able to say that someone else agreed with your decision. These approaches to feedback are not what this book is advocating: they will not help clarify the situation you're dealing with.

If you find yourself strategizing along such lines, let that be a message to explore fear further. Don't bother feeling guilty; guilty thoughts are just another way to avoid being present. In the process of waking ourselves up to genuine presence through mindfulness, we're bound to lapse sometimes. Being willing to recognize mistakes and learn from them is what matters.

We invite further intelligence if, rather than playing the confirmation game when colleagues agree with us, we press for further criticism of our approach. If you feel a colleague may be withholding thoughts out of concern for your feelings, state clearly that critique is what you want, not stroking. If your colleague still hesitates, another approach is to suggest inhabiting the shoes of someone you both know whom you can count on to have a critical approach: What do you think X would say? Addressing the issue in hypothetical terms, through X's mouth, your colleague may feel less personal pressure or embarrassment about being critical.

When you seek critical feedback, make it clear upfront that you're looking for any weaknesses there may be in a particular approach. Courageous leaders—at whatever level they may rank in an organization—are willing to ask that question. So can you.

Mindfulness shows us how being put on the spot can make us hesitate to speak frankly; therefore, when working with others, look for skillful ways to relieve them of that pressure. For example, you may press for critical feedback by couching the process as a joint undertaking, saying, "We both know that there is no single answer to this question, so let's see if you can't tear my conclusion to pieces and then we'll try to put something together that's better." In this way you take responsibility for helping your respondent provide honest feedback.

In professional settings, willingness to be constructively critical is usually seen as an asset: the yes-man is recognized as less likely to make constructive contributions. So you can encourage others to be willing to dissent by emphasizing that what you are really looking for are critical observations; don't simply assume that "it goes without saying" that your colleagues will know that's what you want.

And then, whether your colleague disagrees with your entire conclusion or just certain details, expect to experience the fear feeling again. Even when you've asked for critical feedback, actually getting it is never all that comfortable. Defensiveness (a habitual pattern with a long history) may arise, especially if disagreement is strongly expressed. Mindfulness allows you to see the experience of fear underlying defensiveness, pause, and take it in, connecting with the experience through presence and putting any knee-jerk reaction on hold. It also helps to know that it's not necessary to agree or disagree with feedback immediately; you have no obligation to be reactive. You can simply accept it—gratefully—as further information to take into account.

One of the most valuable insights that comes from practicing mindfulness meditation is that you don't have to identify with your thoughts or with the points of view they provoke; it is possible to identify instead with the more detached awareness presence brings. If you truly internalize that kind of detachment, your relationship to feedback can be the same as if you were acting as an adviser to somebody else—except that in this case that "somebody else" is yourself. You are able to stand outside the situation, so to speak, and take in feedback without defensiveness. You can learn to be your own adviser.

The inverse of defensiveness is a kind of capitulation wherein you think that if someone disagrees with you, they must be right and you must be wrong. Such a crisis of confidence is habitual, just like the defensive reaction, and you don't have to buy into it either. This kind of personal doubt offers valuable information, reflecting as it does how much you believe your own thoughts.

If you have this reaction, take some time when you meditate to be sensitive to the arising of the pattern of self-doubting thoughts. Recognizing it as habitual, a repetitive pattern, undercuts its power to drive your reactions and behaviors. Again, there's no blame attached to this; it's just a part of the empirical process of getting to know yourself better. You may also find it useful to use the contemplation practice described above to explore such doubts.

Risk Assessment

Not only are most people risk averse, even the topic of risk is we tend to shy away from. Like receiving feedback, contemplating risk holds vast potential for triggering the fear feeling, because by its nature risk involves uncertainty, a prime trigger for fear for as long as people have existed. Primitives wondering about the presence of dangerous animals concealed themselves until they could see that the coast was clear; risk assessment and management are hardly new concepts.

But acknowledging and contemplating risk is not a matter of considering (or worse, assuming) that failure is likely; rather, it simply wisdom about relating to the world. We understand that sometimes things don't work out as planned. Uncertainty and risk are facts of life; being willing to face those facts is part of the inner advantage mindfulness imparts. Cultivating mindfulness makes awareness of the fear feeling more accessible; when it arises, simply acknowledge it and apply the three-step fear practice described earlier. This allows you to address risk factors more dispassionately without being pushed into avoidance.

When we are not willing to face facts and engage in practical risk assessment, we may become paralyzed by the prospect of risk. If you find yourself rejecting every idea as too risky, look into whether your reaction to the fear feeling is making you habitually risk-averse.

Another obstacle to pragmatic risk assessment can arise because in the midst of the enthusiasm and excitement that often accompanies a new venture or project, raising the issue of potential challenges—including the possibility of failure— may be perceived as inviting negativity; nevertheless, it is an important part of planning and preparation. One way to approach the possibility of failure from a more positive angle is to look at responsiveness as a matter of agility or resilience: how do you get back on track if setbacks occur?

Similarly, when an organization's objectives are closely tied to a founding entrepreneur's personal vision, raising questions of risk can itself be risky, possibly being interpreted as questioning the boss's intelligence—or displaying disloyalty! Treading diplomatically, but genuinely, requires a mindful approach.

When advocating a new idea—whether it's a product line, a service, a legal strategy, or a marketing campaign—raising the question of what might go wrong may seem like anathema because enthusiasm seems crucial to convincing others of its value. On the other hand, presenting an idea without at least some idea of the potential downside can make the presentation seem ill-considered.

How can we help make sure we don't miss out on dealing with risk factors? The answer is simple: make risk a normal part of the conversation. In the midst of any project, identifying and assessing risk should be on everyone's "to do" list, so that it becomes a customary part of the professional environment. That's no guarantee things won't be missed, but it minimizes the probability of that happening.

Risks come in two varieties: known and unknown. Examples of known risks include whether or not people are going to buy into a particular product or service or idea or politician, whether interest rates are going to go up or down, or how commodity prices will vary. Managing these risks may be a matter of convening focus groups, or hedging financial risks with a reliable counterparty, or buying a futures contract. Although those actions do not totally eliminate risk, they mitigate it.

But there are also unknown risks. How do you hedge against something when you don't know what it is? Obviously there is no simple answer to this conundrum; however, investigating widely all areas of potential concern narrows the window of unknown variables. A risk may be "unknown" to you because you are unfamiliar with a particular situation; that does not mean that no one is aware of the risk or that it is inherently unknowable. Consulting those with breadth and depth of experience is helpful.

For example, the more we know about economic activity in other parts of the world, the more we narrow the window for unknown risks when we are dealing in those areas. The same is true with potential political developments, as governments become more involved in economic activities, whether as borrowers, lenders, venture capitalists, or owners.

Finding yourself considering the possibility of risk is a signal that you are connecting with the practical wisdom of human existence. It need not be depressing—indeed, it can even be exhilarating—to engage mindfully with the possibility of risk. You might even enjoy it.

Because the nature of potential risks may shift as you move through the decision making process, making risk assessment a regular part of your professional activities means assessing risk at several points along the way, and making the last assessment just as you are reaching a final decision. That may be hard because of all the work you've put into the decision-making process before that, but it might be the most valuable exercise of all. As Daniel Kahneman suggests in *Thinking, Fast and Slow*, just before implementing the final decision, do a "pre-mortem": project yourself a year later and assume that the project has failed (or hasn't lived up to expectations). See what that tells you.

Physicist Niels Bohr is reputed to have said, "Prediction is difficult, especially about the future." Inevitably, in dealing with risk, we're dealing with uncertainties that are facts of life, and accurately predicting their occurrence is no sure thing. But by relating to the world with mindfulness—using fear as a powerful ally—you can confront risk in a sane and balanced way, neither ignoring it nor being paralyzed by it. Uncertainty becomes part of the atmosphere, like water to a fish.

Timing

"Timing is everything" is a truism that is crucially relevant under many conditions. Don't ask your boss for a raise when the company's finances are in the tank, unless you precede your request with a convincing plan for saving the company's bacon. Don't propose major organizational restructuring when the company is about to introduce a significant new product or service, unless you've got a really good reason.

Regardless of the details of a situation, asking if this is the right time to implement a project or strategy is almost always going to be relevant, especially with emphasis on risk evaluation, whether operational, strategic, or financial. Even if the answer appears obvious, it can't hurt to raise the question, because what initially seems obvious isn't always so convincing once you examine it further. Other times the issue of timing is off the table, such as when the boss, client, or customer says, "Do it—now!"

Skill in addressing timing issues requires overcoming two principal obstacles: speed and procrastination. Speed pushes us to do it now, do it fast. Procrastination slows us down without good reason. Bringing mindfulness to the situation helps us overcome both of these obstacles.

Recognizing the charged-up feeling of a speedy mind, we can use it as a helpful reminder to take a break, pause, and ask, "Why the rush? Does it really have to happen now?" If so, then so be it. But instead of letting the speedy feeling accompany your activity, pause in presence for a moment. Speedy mind really doesn't help, so let it go. As Marc Lesser points out in LESS: *Accomplishing More by Doing Less*, there is a big difference between *being* busy and *feeling* busy.

Procrastination, the reluctance to take action or come to a decision, is often the result of not relating mindfully with the fear feeling. When we haven't learned how to deal with the fear feeling, a fight, flight, or freeze reaction may kick in. Hesitating to "pull the trigger" on an action or decision is an example of the freeze reaction. For example, most of us are familiar with the experience of needing (or wanting) to make a telephone call but finding it difficult to pick up the phone and dial the number. As part of your mindfulness training, reflect on that experience, and notice whether you experience the fear feeling. You may also recognize the reasons you give yourself to rationalize delaying the call.

At that point also let go of any story line you may be telling yourself to justify procrastination. Stay with the energizing feeling of fear, and then act. You don't have to get rid of the fear feeling or wait until it goes away; you can act at the same time you experience the fear; being present with fear as you act is an expression of dynamic equanimity. Of course, there may be a genuine reason to delay the call, but don't avoid it out of fear-based procrastination.

Timing is a relevant consideration in the steps leading to any primary objective. But if the timing issue is hijacked by speed or procrastination, you may never get around to addressing it. A more productive alternative is to routinely ask yourself and your colleagues relevant questions about timing. For example, you might discuss such issues as, When is the latest we can make the decision and still be able to implement it on schedule? Asking this is not promoting procrastination but merely opening up the space for new information or insights. A lot can happen between now and later. If you make the decision too soon, you may pass up opportunities to refine and improve your choices.

Communicating Decisions

Communicating decisions requires that you consider clarity, completeness (that is, just how much to say), timing, confidentiality, and the overriding question of who makes the final call about communication. If you are the ultimate decision-maker, it all comes together with you—the substance of the decision itself and how it's communicated, whether by you or by someone to whom you've delegated the task. If you're not in charge, make sure you understand your role in the process and don't make assumptions.

Be conscious of the intended audience in formulating the communication. Should you be communicating the decision only or will lots of detail be required? Will the recipient want details in advance, to be followed by an informed discussion of the conclusions drawn? If the communication is a press conference or press release announcing a new product or service, then the communication will focus more on selling the idea than explaining the ins and outs of making the decision.

When a decision has great significance, issues of timing and confidentiality are front and center. Introducing a new product line, closing an old plant, spinning off a division, or filling a significant post in the organization all call for careful consideration of who knows what about the decision and when. If potential negotiations are likely—as is often the case with major decisions—you may face decisions involving not only the ultimate objective but also the negotiating strategy for getting there.

Even a thoughtful decision, if it is not well communicated, can result in disaster, with repercussions not only for the organization but for the individuals involved. Thus communicating a decision is not just an incidental trifle but requires an understanding of the entire situation. Whether your personal style is concise or verbose, training in mindfulness will help you gain clarity so that you can get an overview of the situation and see what's called for.

Communication

C ommunication is risky business. In the ancient literary tradition of the comedy of errors, the central plot device involves miscommunication, either by characters not saying what they really think or by their saying something that's misunderstood. But what is amusing on the stage is less so in the business place, where people may miscommunicate for reasons ranging from accepted social patterns (Some things just aren't mentioned in polite company!) to individual incompetence or manipulation. Some people attribute miscommunication to gender differences, biology, socialization, or distinctions of class or status. But whatever the context, the inherent riskiness of communication is seldom overtly acknowledged. Communication—which, like other risks, involves uncertainty—triggers fear.

In addition, communication can invoke an entire range of other emotions—from sadness, to anger, to joy—sometimes described as the "tone" of the interaction. Familiarity with emotions allows us to connect with the totality of what is going on. It's not that emotion is more important than reason; rather, it's that, although we may not be aware of it, we rarely experience one totally divorced from the other. Thoughts have a perceptible "feel" to them, and feelings are often accompanied by thoughts. Depending on your personal style, you may emphasize one or the other, but in applying mindfulness, you need to recognize that they're a package. Otherwise you fragment your perception of the situation and relate to it only partially.

In discussing communication, we will address three activities:

✧ *listening and speaking*
✧ *diplomacy*
✧ *negotiation*

Listening and Speaking

Interpersonal communication can be seen from two perspectives: that of the speaker and that of the listener. It generally works best between two people when they alternate the roles. Applying mindfulness makes that easier.

From the listener's point of view, applying mindfulness involves both outward mindfulness and inward mindfulness. Outwardly, the question is whether you can listen to the speaker without being distracted. Do you find yourself spaced out or daydreaming? When you are distracted, not only do you fail to hear the speaker's words, you may also miss subtler cues that the speaker is communicating, intentionally or not. These might include fear and nervousness, desperation, impatience, sadness, light-heartedness, or others.

Distraction can also keep you from noticing how a speaker communicates. Mumbling or dropping certain words can communicate the speaker's mindset. On the other hand, fixating too intently upon the words can also be a form of distraction. Intense focus may give you the impression that you are not distracted, but it is different from the state of relaxed awareness described in this book as mindful presence. Likewise, being so engrossed with the tone communicated that you miss the words means your connection with the situation is also limited.

Inward mindfulness involves awareness of one's own emotional responses to the speaker. If you attend only to the words and the tone being communicated by the speaker, while ignoring your own responses, you're still only relating partially to the situation. For example, do you feel drawn to what is being said? If not, do you feel repelled or simply uncertain?

At this point, you should just listen and feel the response. If you try to analyze the feeling (Do I like this situation? Am I being manipulated? Do I find this threatening?), you are just getting distracted by your thoughts again. Simply notice the feeling; you can always revisit it later if that would be useful.

For the listener, the expectation of having to respond to the speaker can kick start the fear feeling. So recognizing and staying with the fear feeling can help you stay engaged in a fluid way in a conversation. It's rare that you have to express your reaction immediately, and it's often valuable to wait so as to avoid cutting off the conversation or offending the speaker. If a response seems required, "I see" usually works pretty well.

Now let's switch to the perspective of the speaker. The speaker's role is both opportunity and challenge. The opportunity is to establish both the terms of the discussion and its tone. The challenge is that either the terms or the tone might be rejected by the listener. Because of the fear feeling, the speaker may experience a heightened momentum of thoughts, which may in turn affect the speaker's speech, resulting in oversharing, awkward phrasing, or unintentionally adopting either a harsh or weak tone.

Cultivating inward mindfulness helps the speaker avoid these pitfalls. Momentum can also undermine a speaker's outward mindfulness, keeping him or her so wrapped up in thoughts or in speaking that the listener's responses go unnoticed. Is the listener engaged by what is being said, or bored, or offended? Outward mindfulness will help the speaker avoid losing track of the listener.

The experience of presence cultivated through meditation can be a boon to a speaker, who can connect with it before launching a presentation. Even if you're nervous, you can appreciate the reliability of your natural presence, fostering further confidence.

Speakers sometimes pause because they've been told it's a good thing to do, but strategized pausing can come across as artificial. A pause needn't be ostentatious or protracted, perhaps just the length of a smile or a hello, and presence makes such a pause feel more natural and relaxing. Mindful pausing feels natural because it is natural, an expression of presence: Here we are. It is the exact opposite of being frozen by fear. It may even have the effect of helping the listener relax and be more present. Relaxation can occur because mindful pausing cuts through momentum and allows the speaker to acknowledge the listener, knowing the challenges of being the listener.

This discussion of communication has emphasized applying mindfulness to perceptions. "Perception," as we're using the term here, is very different from the popular use of "perception" in the press, especially in the political press. In the media "perception" is often used to put a spin or interpretation on certain events. You might read, "There was nothing really wrong with what she did, but it gave the perception of blah blah blah." This is a form of deception that lets the speaker attack while appearing sympathetic. Mindfulness helps us see through this kind of rhetoric and encourages clarity in our own perception of communication.

Diplomacy

Applying mindfulness to diplomacy involves fostering three sets of values:

✧ *empathy*
✧ *integrity*
✧ *sophistication*

Empathy

In this discussion, empathy refers to the activity of appreciating the position (in the sense of interests, desires, and needs) of another individual or group. In popular parlance, empathy is the ability to "stand in their shoes," or "look at it from the other person's point of view."

The principal obstacle to empathy is self-absorption. If you are constantly focused on yourself, it's hard to see a situation from another's perspective. Narcissists filter facts, seeking implications for how they will be affected. This habitual offender counters any opposition with something like, "How could he do this to me?" or "What did I do to make her act like that?" By contrast, responding with empathy might involve asking, "I wonder where she's coming from?" Or "Did I do something to offend you?"

The tendency toward self-absorption is undercut by regular exposure to the practice of meditation. The opportunity to witness how your thoughts continually arise and notice their content makes it hard to miss how often they have to do with "me": what happened to me in the past and what will happen to me in the future. In my wife's felicitous phrase, we are constantly "rehashing and rehearsing," rehashing the past and rehearsing the future. Self-involvement is tedious and stressful but you can cut through it if you're brave enough to identify your own style of self-involvement so that you can recognize when it happens.

Although we usually think about empathy in relation to others, it can also apply to ourselves. This can be particularly helpful in cutting through assumptions about our motivations. For example, if you find yourself being particularly self-righteous, applying self-empathy may reveal that your principled statement masks an unacknowledged interest in the outcome of the situation. Not only is that insight clarifying, but it may also save you the embarrassment of having it pointed out when you have been on your high horse too long.

Self-empathy may also reveal an unacknowledged assumption about what you *ought* to be doing, a frequent theme of the guilt-ridden; seeing the assumption may help you investigate why you're making it in the first place. It may also reveal self-doubt, which you can examine so that it doesn't block a more realistic assessment of your capabilities.

Integrity

The second value belies the old saying, "An ambassador is an honest gentleman sent abroad to lie for his country." Despite being witty, the saying is overly cynical because acting diplomatically—whether on a personal or geopolitical level—usually has the object of securing someone's cooperation or non-opposition. If what we say is not taken seriously because our integrity is suspect, we may fail to accomplish our objective.

Issues of integrity come up on a number of levels, from facts, to interpretations, to intentions. With any of these, mindfulness can be useful in testing your assumptions and motivations.

Take facts, for example. Situations involving factual integrity are sometimes fairly straightforward; the facts are simple and known to us. If you say that you did or did not do something that is not the case, who will believe you next time? The story of the little boy who cried wolf is a relevant parable. We would, of course, like to think that we would never do such a thing, but sometimes facts are embarrassing, either in themselves or by virtue of our having been caught out or having demonstrated an unfortunate lapse of judgment that the facts of the matter lay clear. In the words of John Adams, "Facts are stubborn things."

Embarrassment, as a manifestation of fear, can lead us into deceptive behaviors; however, if we have trained ourselves to ride the energy of fear, then, when confronted with an embarrassing fact, the feeling of fear can remind us to pause—resting in the open space of presence—rather than to launch a knee-jerk response. Although we might wish not to have engaged in the exposed act itself, at this point, what's done is done. No need to make it worse.

In the realm of interpretations, issues of integrity become subtler. Actions and words are often ambiguous; if you ignore the ambiguity of someone's actions or words, you may fool yourself into thinking something was clear when it wasn't. For example, you may want very much to believe that someone has agreed with you when their statement was actually hedged, perhaps because they didn't want to seem uncooperative. In such an instance fear is operating on both ends of the conversation. The other person didn't want to disagree, fearing your disappointment. And you, wanting to believe that the other person was agreeing and not wanting to confront possible refusal, interpreted a conditional statement as unequivocal.

But it doesn't have to be that way. If you've trained yourself to recognize and stay with the fear feeling, you can engage the situation mindfully. Detecting a hedged statement ("I'll see" or "Maybe so"), there are several possibilities for you to move forward. You can simply say you're not sure whether the two of you have agreed. Or if the person habitually speaks in hedged language (we lawyers can be prone to that approach), you may find that he or she is actually willing to agree if pressed. If you find that the person is not sure right now but is willing to get back to you, you can say when you need to know. Or you may discover that the person simply doesn't agree, in which case you've got your answer, avoiding a lot of misunderstanding and wasted time. You may not feel great about it, but you knew you were taking a chance by asking. What is key is not to indulge in wishful thinking, avoiding a clear answer out of fear.

If, instead, you present what is ambiguous as clear, your opposite number may view you as manipulative, dishonest, or stupid. Saying "You agreed" may be countered by, "No I didn't; I said it was worth considering. You know that!" Thus a lack of clarity can poison future encounters, making others wary of dealing with us. Also, some people try to appear stupid as a way of gaining advantage; if this is discerned, it at best raises questions: "Is he really stupid, or is he just trying to jerk me around? I'd better be careful."

These examples illustrate the desirability of approaching any situation with an attitude of genuineness (another word for "integrity"), examining your motivations and assumptions critically through mindfulness: Do I really know what I am asserting to be the case? Can I clearly and honestly say, if only to myself, what I want out of the situation?

Answering questions like these is challenging if what you really want from the situation is inconsistent with your self-image. You need to decide: am I being motivated by an emotional upheaval, perhaps liking or disliking the opposite party? What assumptions have I made about the motivation of the "other side"? Am I only in this for the money, even though I'd rather not admit that motivation to myself? Contemplating questions such as these mindfully can bring clarity to your interactions and integrity to your communications.

Sophistication

"Sophistication" is another word with many meanings and connotations; however, the Greek root of the word refers to wisdom. Wisdom is different from knowledge, which has to do with understanding facts, language, social structures, and other "observables"; in contrast, wisdom has to do with having a sense of how events of a certain kind tend to unfold, how diverse motivations tend to interact, and with other dynamics that are hard to quantify. It is usually born of experience, which is why smart entrepreneurs often seek out a mentor with a depth of experience. Professional advisers can also fill this role because of their exposure to a wide variety of analogous situations.

Knowledge of the world, its history, economics, literature, science, and political and social structures help inform wisdom; however, getting too deeply immersed in details can result in "not seeing the forest for the trees." Because every situation, however similar to others, is unique, you will be thrown back on making judgment calls which inevitably involve uncertainty, the reliable generator of fear. Wisdom recognizes that trying to avoid fear by rushing to a quick solution may cause you to miss realizing that you are dealing with a judgment call rather than established fact.

Mindfulness meditation can help bring wisdom into our activities. It can help us recognize questionable assumptions. By seeing how we react negatively to certain actions or words, we will tend to avoid inflicting them on others if we're seeking agreement. Or we may notice ourselves responding rigidly if we feel boxed in by an argument or situation; if we're trying to help an opponent be flexible, we avoid rigidity triggers. Sophistication involves understanding how to work with everyday patterns of human interaction skillfully.

Negotiation

Whatever the subject matter of a negotiation, it helps not to be at the mercy of your habitual patterns. Being present and attentive are qualities the negotiator needs. The perils of being distracted during a negotiation are obvious. When habitual patterns control us, we may miss cues and hints. Also, if our distractedness manifests outwardly, it may give the impression that our heart is not in the negotiation, so others presume we may be easily pressed for concessions.

Ungoverned nervousness can result in speaking "filler" or ill-considered language, from which you have to backtrack, weakening your position. If your mind is speedy—another fear reaction—you may seem impatient to reach a resolution, which can encourage the other side to push or resist more. If you have learned how to harness the fear feeling, you will be more energized and engaged with the conversation.

In my professional life I've been involved in negotiations that included many complex business and financial arrangements, in the course of which I've come to appreciate and enjoy the fact that negotiation is the blend of the analytical with the playful. Negotiations portrayed in the movies and television are almost invariably high-tension situations; although those do sometimes occur, business negotiations aren't usually "bet the company" situations and therefore lend themselves to more flexible approaches. Getting comfortable with the uncertainties of negotiations will allow you to relax alertly and enjoy the sparring, without losing track of your objective.

Since negotiations are unpredictable, even if you've prepared thoroughly, the other negotiator may raise an unexpected issue. You may get lucky and negotiate successfully from an unprepared position, but the situation is not optimal. If you're unwilling to temporize because of a rigid self-image—"I'm the kind of person who can handle anything"—well, good luck to you; but if you have examined your underlying self-image mindfully, you can avoid getting stuck that way. Recognizing the unexpected, you can pause and take stock rather than react automatically. It may be time to take a break and confer with your team or put the issue on a list of open items.

Sometimes you may harbor negative attitudes toward the other side or toward a member of their negotiating team, and these feelings might make it difficult to reach agreement. Developing self-awareness can help you avoid being trapped in mindsets that bias your approach. Don't forget that you're engaged in negotiation because you want to find a resolution, not to torpedo it, even if the context of the negotiation is unfriendly.

Similarly, explore whether you hold unhelpful attitudes about people on your own side of the table. If you do, recognize and let them go before you walk into the room. Squabbles among allies in a negotiation are not only unprofessional but embarrassing and counterproductive.

In any negotiation, an important question is, Who is the decision-maker? There is not always a single answer to this; it may depend on the issue. The job of a negotiating team may be, rather than to reach a final decision, to work the negotiation "range" into as favorable a position as possible, so that the boss can step in at the last session to work out the final, momentous issues. Even on points for which the negotiating team does have decision-making authority, it may be advantageous to assert the need to consult with someone who's not present at the table—a trick car dealers have long used to their advantage—or with the team privately. In today's digital world, a team member may even text the others to suggest a break.

In some circumstances no one other than the CEO may know what the ultimate desired outcome—say, the price—is. And although he or she may instruct negotiators about an acceptable range of outcomes, privately there may be a "worst case" result that he or she won't even disclose to the negotiating team. Knowing the worst acceptable case might prejudice the negotiators toward a quick result rather than holding out for a better one.

Make sure you understand clearly your role in the negotiation. Are you the speaker, strategist, or observer? If you have any question about this, clarify your responsibilities in pre-negotiation meetings with your team. All these functions are valuable, even though the speaker may seem to have the starring role. Don't let your self-image lead you into incorrect assumptions about the position you're playing.

Sometimes our instructions as negotiators may require taking an uncomfortable position; it can be helpful to exercise your mindfulness muscles to be aware of how you're feeling about that. If you don't, your discomfort may unconsciously communicate an attitude of uncertainty that undermines your position; however, if you can acknowledge the discomfort to yourself, you can explore the reasons for it, with a colleague if necessary, and either change position or find a way to accommodate it. If you have cultivated your ability to remain undistractedly present, you can negotiate effectively, even outside your comfort zone. As a member of a negotiating team (particularly in the observer role), you also want to be sensitive about whether any members of the opposing team seem uncomfortable with the position they're taking; that could provide a basis for pressing a concession successfully.

In pre-negotiation planning you'll have addressed the likely negotiating range of the other side. Of course whatever you conclude is only a beginning, to be refined as negotiations proceed. If you're operating undistractedly, you may observe a number of cues that the other side inadvertently communicates. Perhaps they're hesitant about a particular point or, conversely, they may exhibit bluster and oversell in an unconvincing way. The ability to remain present (especially being bluster-resistant) facilitates observation. Even though it may be impossible to know for certain the other side's position, if you probe you may find for further information.

One of the biggest challenges in negotiations is dealing with a highly aggressive opponent. Aggressive behavior is intended to provoke a response, so the ability to remain present and avoid reactivity is valuable. I recall a negotiation where one of the negotiators was very aggressive, almost abusive. Someone else at the table looked at the person, smiled, and said "You're good," indicating that he recognized gamesmanship when he saw it. The offender immediately turned the volume down. It's hard to keep pushing when nobody's pushing back.

Your mindfulness muscles can help you investigate whether you are motivated to find creative solutions when negotiations seem blocked. Negotiation is not simply about splitting the difference, and offering a split may be perceived as a sign of over-willingness to compromise, prompting the other side to push harder. However, if you go into a negotiation stuck in an adversarial mindset, you'll miss opportunities for resolution. Using negotiation to find out what the other side really values can reveal potential tradeoffs. The contemplation technique discussed in the decision-making portion of Part Three (and in Appendix 3) can help you explore these possibilities.

Finally, consider the possibility of not reaching agreement. The prospect of failure may be fearsome, triggering an angry response from your superiors or dissolving into litigation; however, don't let fear keep you from examining these possibilities. Be sure your team is aware of them, as they may incentivize an imaginative resolution with the other side. On the other hand, the prospect that you may walk away from the table may trigger concessions from the adversary; so in addition to considering what the failure to reach agreement means for your side, consider whether the consequences for the opposition are even greater.

Creativity

C reativity is one of those "big deal" words. When we use it, we may think of Picasso, or Shakespeare, or Einstein. But even those of us not in that august company have valuable skills and talents that lend themselves to creativity. Particularly in areas of professional activity, we face challenges involving surprises, problems, and situations for which we have no routine solution and which present the opportunity to marshal our resourcefulness.

Creativity is sometimes called for in dealing with situations that superficially seem routine. For example a new financial instrument requires creativity to identify the array of implications to be addressed. By the umpteenth time it is used, familiar transaction structures, templates, and forms will likely have been developed at which point the creativity challenge shifts to looking for aspects of the transaction that require adjusting; one of the classic hazards of standardization is the potential for numbing us to needed adaptations. Mindfulness helps use see when creativity is called for, and it also can help us make it happen.

The effects of mindfulness on creativity fall into three categories:

✧ *insight (individual creativity)*
✧ *intuition (the gut check)*
✧ *collaboration (group creativity)*

Insight: Cultivating Individual Creativity

When our minds are full of busyness, there isn't much space for insight to arise. The contemplation technique described in Part Three can change that, helping us address novel situations, especially those with no obvious solution.

A few minutes of contemplation can lead to a new perspective or approach. Cicero, the ancient Roman, said, "Only the person who is relaxed can create, and to that mind ideas flow like lightning." In the context of this book, we would paraphrase Cicero to say, "To the person who is present, ideas flow like lightning."

With this contemplation technique, insight will often arise in the form of a thought. Therefore, the value of becoming familiar with the thinking process—and especially its habitual manifestation—is that you are familiar enough with that process that you can identify thoughts that add value, thoughts we call "insights."

As professionals we often have a bias in favor of do it now, do it fast, get it done; however, that isn't necessarily the best approach—it's just one of those preconceptions or assumptions that we can learn to see for what it is. And yes, just sitting there doing "nothing" can open up the space for creative insight to appear.

To give an example from a professional context, I used contemplation in a situation in which my client was dealing with multiple other parties. They had ongoing disputes with each other but not with my client; nevertheless, the result was that it was difficult to obtain cooperation to resolve the situation. Having talked with my client about this frustrating situation, I later closed my door and simply sat quietly, letting the question of how to resolve the situation float. For quite some time nothing much happened; then abruptly an insight popped up: just wait, nothing has to happen right now.

Sometimes doing nothing can indeed be the best way forward. But having that insight is just the starting point. Insights, like other bits of information, are most valuable when they are examined critically; the fact of having had one doesn't necessarily mean it's the final answer. So having had the "just wait" insight, the next task in my story was to explore it.

Could the solution simply wait? I didn't know any reason it couldn't, so I talked it over with the client, who agreed.

In case you're wondering how the waiting game turned out, everything slowed down, and then the financial crisis of the late 2000s intervened. Waiting turned out to be not only an appropriate response, given the circumstances with the other parties, but fortunate. A project was put on hold that might have been a financial disaster had it gone forward.

On another occasion, I was advising a client who was at loggerheads with an adjoining property owner. My client was intent on purchasing the property, and the adjoiner was just as adamant about staying there for the rest of his life. He was willing to have his estate deed over the property on his death (even to providing for that in his will), but my client wisely recognized that such arrangements sometimes were frustrated, either by a change in the will or by resistance from the owner's executor or heirs.

Recognizing that neither was going to give up his position, I spent some time in contemplation and a solution occurred to me: have the owner deed the property to my client now and, in the deed, reserve the use of the property for as long as the owner lived, an arrangement known as a "life estate". Everyone was happy: the seller lived there contently until his death, after which my client was able to repurpose the property to meet his own business needs.

Insights can also arise unbidden. One morning during sitting meditation, I had an idea that was relevant to a project I was working on. In that case, it wasn't central to the project itself but related to how to present it so others would be open to it. I hadn't considered the presentation issue, but once the insight had occurred, it informed the approach in a way that made the project work better. It had been one of those unknown variables.

Caveat: don't expect a payoff every time you practice meditation or contemplation. Still you can appreciate the pleasant surprises. Even if you sit for just ten minutes at a time, cultivating presence through meditation can help slow you down enough so that you notice where an innovative application of contemplative practice might be useful.

However, although Cicero credits relaxation with triggering creativity, you may very well find yourself in a situation where relaxation through meditation and/or contemplation isn't an option. In those situations, being present is the best alternative. If you are in a meeting with lots of people talking, simply reconnect with the experience of presence. Often this only requires remembering to be present, perhaps triggered by noticing that you're distracted.

Finding some open space in the midst of what seems like chaos—even if that space is only within your mind— can reestablish your connection with presence. Then, even if no particular insight arises, you will have awarded yourself a few moments of a spacious state of mind. Who knows? You might hear something that you otherwise would have missed.

Intuition (The Gut Check)

If there is one thing I have a clear intuition about, it is that this topic requires some definition. So, before exploring how intuition may be relevant in professional applications, let's define what we're talking about.

Daniel Kahneman has described "intuition" as "knowing but without knowing how you know." In a discussion of mindfulness, that's actually a useful definition because the uncertainty factor highlights the potential for the fear feeling, making us nervous, uncomfortable. Maybe we'd be more comfortable calling it a "gut check."

Used in many different contexts, ranging from scientific discovery to premonitions and other ESP experiences, intuition has been studied in the fields of psychology, economics, and decision-making. In the context of diplomacy, as our earlier discussion about empathy—sensing the needs and motivations of others—suggests, intuition can be relevant. Intuition is also central to creativity, where we deliberately open so insights may arise.

People who are hyper-rational often have trouble with intuition because it flies in the face of their self-image. Exposure to meditation helps to undermine fixed ideas about ourselves so we become more comfortable with a variety of inner experiences. Still, acknowledging and expressing an intuition in a semi-public setting such as a meeting or negotiation is more challenging than simply feeling it when practicing meditation.

Kahneman devotes a good deal of discussion to what he calls "expert intuition." In a given situation you might be considered the "expert" because of individual talents or experiences; sometimes an organization will recruit an outside expert to provide a perspective separate from those who have been intimately involved.

In that context, Kahneman is particularly interested in how we decide whether to rely on the intuition of the expert. Obviously, it goes beyond simply saying that, well, we paid for it so we'd better use it. (Believe it or not, that happens!) Kahneman believes that expert intuitions are a function of pattern recognition based on memory, even if the intuiter can't identify the source. Because of the memory connection, he suggests two criteria to create the likelihood of validation. The operative word here is "likelihood"; the ultimate validation depends on whether reliance on the intuition is confirmed by the outcome.

The first criterion is whether the environment in which the intuition is operating is sufficiently regular or predictable. If the environment contains too many variables, intuition may be suspect. If the criterion of regularity is established, the second criterion is whether the intuiter has had adequate opportunity to become familiar with the environment.

Mindfulness can be helpful when exploring "expert intuition." For example, you might find it difficult to question the expert's authority, especially if the expert has a previous relationship to your organization or its executives or owners; however, willingness to stay with the fear feeling and not clam up will help you stay engaged and possibly even come up with a skillful way to investigate the expertise diplomatically.

Training in mindfulness can also help cue you as to when it might be a good idea to curb your enthusiasm for your own intuition, at least long enough to inquire into its validity. It is entirely possible to have a strong "intuition" about a topic and be totally wrong—another educational experience. A little humility goes a long way.

Mindful Collaboration: Getting to Best

Collaboration is like negotiation in that both involve interactions with others and communication skills, resolution of issues, and arriving at conclusions. In a fundamental way, however, they are different. In negotiation, the parties are attempting to reach a *modus vivendi*, either a way to work together in the future, or a way of resolving a dispute so that they no longer have to relate to each other, at least with respect to that particular situation.

Collaboration has to do with working together to address a particular objective, and the point of the exercise is to bring about a superior result. As such, collaboration can be viewed as a method for enhancing group creativity. To achieve that result, parties often collaborate because they bring different kinds of technical expertise or other resources to bear or because each brings a depth of judgment or experience the other does not.

Sometimes there can be overlap between negotiation and collaboration; for example, the parties are negotiating what they hope will be a long-term relationship, and at the same time they want the results of that relationship to be as excellent as possible. Or a party may introduce a feeling of collaboration into a negotiation as a technique to induce the other to take softer positions.

Working with groups, I use four principles of mindful collaboration to stimulate group creativity. These are not steps in collaboration but rather are attitudes or techniques you can bring to the collaborative process.

Explore Other Perspectives

Recognition of the value of exploring varied perspectives grows out of the self-awareness cultivated by mindfulness; in particular, you become aware that particular styles or techniques are comfortable for you. They come naturally to you, and through them you've often functioned successfully. Conversely, in working with others, you become aware of differing styles or perspectives.

To prepare for collaboration, you need not only to do your own homework and analysis, but you also need to make a point of deliberately exploring the topic from one or more perspectives you've observed in others. If you're a "feeler," someone always interested in how others are likely to respond to a situation, consider the topic from the point of view of an "analyzer," someone who prefers to dissect a thought and evaluate it from a logical perspective, or vice versa. Or, if you tend to look at the politics of a situation—how it will play with various individuals or groups in the organization, from the boss to a variety of stakeholders—consider other perspectives, such as social or environment implications, as well as how you would articulate them.

Don't Be Afraid of Your Own Perspective

Sometimes people misunderstand the suggestion to explore other perspectives as somehow devaluing or diminishing their own perspective; therefore, as a corrective, here is the second principle of mindful collaboration—don't be afraid to express your own perspective. After all, if the object of collaboration is the sharing of intelligence, judgment, and experience, it benefits no one if people hold back. Be alert to the operation of the fear feeling about expressing your approach in the face of differences, without becoming intimidated simply because others may not see it the same way.

Don't Be Afraid of an Untested Idea

In the course of collaborative conversations, an idea may occur to you that you have not thought about before. You may not even be certain that the idea is one you would ultimately subscribe to. If you are bound by fearful mind, you won't share the idea because you think it might make you look foolish. This behavior will impoverish the conversation; in the interest of genuine collaboration, simply put it out there. You may even preface it by saying, "Here's an idea that I'm not even sure I agree with, but it might be worth exploring."

Questions Trump Statements

People often believe that strength lies in asserting positions, but it's more helpful in stimulating collaborative discussions to ask questions. If you have a position you want explored, it may facilitate conversation to phrase it as a question. Your fellow collaborators may feel less hesitation if they do not hear the assertion as one in which you are personally invested.

∞

The purpose of these principles is to encourage a flow of collaboration so that as much intelligence and wisdom as possible are exchanged, including intuitions. Think about how collaboration would be likely to unfold if the *opposite* approaches were applied: not considering other perspectives makes it more difficult for the collaborator to see the possible wisdom in them; holding back your own perspective deprives others of the benefit of your insights; fearing to raise an untested idea may squander an opportunity for the collaboration to reach superior conclusions; and avoiding the softer approach of questioning rather than assertion may turn the collaboration into a battle of points of view.

Mindfulness promotes this kind of collaboration because as we cultivate self-awareness, we have a better chance of recognizing whether something "inside" may be getting in the way. As suggested throughout this book, learning to work with fear is essential to avoid being walled in by habitual reactions. If you're willing to communicate without the heaviness of habitual hesitation, your engagement in collaboration will be more playful, more creative and more enjoyable for yourself and others.

Leadership

Practically every human activity involving more than one person involves leadership. We are exercising leadership whenever we seek to influence the direction or outcome of any situation in which we are engaged. When we couple mindfulness with leadership, we see how presence allows us to engage genuinely and influence without coercion.

This discussion of how we might join the insights of mindfulness practice with leadership will address:

❖ *authenticity*

❖ *encouraging excellence*

Authenticity

Mindful self-awareness has been part of leadership studies for many years. Almost two decades ago management authority Peter Drucker observed that before you can manage others effectively, you have to be able to manage yourself. Self-management calls for the kind of self-awareness cultivated in mindfulness meditation; mindfulness also helps foster authenticity in a leader, because self-awareness is a touchstone, the starting point for cultivating emotional and social intelligence.

On a superficial level, an authentic leader (or authentic person, for that matter) is one who is not a fraud, who is not pretending to be someone other than who he or she actually is. Of course, in some situations, people will defend their own unproductive or obnoxious behavior by saying, "That's just who I am." And who can argue with that? However, in attempting to propagate a vision of authentic leadership, we're looking for something deeper, based in the wisdom of mindfulness rather than in the habitual patterns of a lifetime.

If "being oneself" just consists of reproducing habitual patterns, it's unlikely to inspire respect and confidence; therefore, a wise move for a leader or one who aspires to lead would be to engage in personal introspection and become familiar with habitual patterns, the thought processes that distract us from being in the present. Because of this, mindfulness has become a significant part of many leadership training programs as well as executive coaching.

As we've discussed earlier, common obstacles to being present include defensiveness, the kind of thinking that attempts to ward off criticism rather than to learn from it, and constantly viewing events with a negative or critical eye, being inclined to see a problem in virtually every situation. Another obstacle involves manipulating others to our cause or project by employing the communication strategies of being seductive, or schmoozy, as well as indifference, in which we don't care to know the views of others or automatically doubt that they have value.

Identifying your personal style, even on such gross levels, can be a helpful starting point in exploring authenticity personally. The subtleties will come along later—walk before you run. Mindfulness meditation is an effective tool for this kind of exploration because it is an empirical investigation: you simply look at and recognize patterns without trying to change them. Your perception is enhanced by not getting involved in evaluation (another form of conceptual distraction), not judging the patterns as good or bad, beneficial or destructive. You have to recognize what's going on before you can become an effective judge of its value. This approach expresses deep trust that you can recognize what's worth cultivating and what's not. It also helps you learn how to further rest in simple presence.

Natural presence, the perfect ground for authentic leadership, seems to come to some people fairly effortlessly. A former law partner of mine was a fine example of this. Herbert was unobtrusively brilliant and his career demonstrated it. During World War Two he had a role in military intelligence; previously he had graduated from Harvard, both as an undergraduate student and a law student. He was completely at ease within himself, and his counsel was much valued by his clients. Herbert became my unofficial mentor. I suspect he didn't think of himself that way, but in my mind there was no doubt. His attention to detail made him not only an excellent attorney but also a remarkable amateur photographer.

His ability to listen and make connections on all fronts and his reputation as a man of integrity led many to seek him out; he was particularly pleased to have been chosen as a principal adviser to the estate of Margaret Mitchell, the author of *Gone with the Wind*. But he was never too busy to lend an ear, and a hand, if possible; when my wife wrote her first book, he offered an introduction to Margaret Mitchell's literary agent. Whether he ever did anything he would have called meditation, I don't know, but I do know his presence was palpable and inspired me to want to emulate him.

To do that, I had to explore my own inner world. I used the practices suggested in this book as a tool to do that. Mindfulness meditation exposes you to the raw material of your patterns. Then you can use the contemplation practice to explore those patterns further, to encourage insight about those patterns. Just remember that these two techniques have different objectives, so it's most productive to do them separately.

Observing in meditation the repetitive quality of thoughts tends to undermine their credibility. After all, seeing them as a tape loop, especially when they have no relevance to present experience, exposes them as space fillers, like leaving the television on while no one's watching. You also begin to discern the difference between habitual thinking and thinking that is consciously undertaken. As familiarity grows, you recognize these qualities more and more in everyday circumstances, allowing you to more fully inhabit every moment of your life.

From the perspective of mindfulness, the opposite of authenticity is not deliberate falsehood but habit. Loosened from the patterns of habit, the mindful leader is open, flexible, and inquisitive—qualities that naturally arise out of mindfulness—rather than walled off, rigid, and arrogant.

Usually, excellent leaders are perceived by others as functioning out of deeply held values and motivations. Once you start to clear the underbrush of habitual thinking and emotional reactivity, you can see more clearly what you truly care about and examine your commitment to the value of whatever product or service you may be offering. If you find that commitment lacking, leadership in that organization is probably not right for you. If that commitment is present, mindfulness can help enable you to work more skillfully. Use the two techniques of meditation and contemplation to explore your values so that your actions as a leader reflect your genuine motivations.

Encouraging Excellence

Excellence doesn't mean trying to be the best at everything. Anyone who has achieved excellence in a particular endeavor knows the tremendous amount of effort that takes. Only after we have built the foundation for excellence through effort can we respond flexibly and creatively to challenging situations. And people who have achieved excellence often find that knowing a lot about one topic or activity exposes how little they know about so many others—a genuine expression of humility that can inspire further inquiry as well as collaboration.

An attitude of excellence means mindfully approaching any job, project, or other situation with the intention of doing your best. Cultivating that attitude deliberately, taking a grounded approach, recognizing what is within the resources available to you, and setting reasonable priorities does not mean you never push beyond the conventionally "realistic" but that when you do, you do so with full comprehension of potential and risk.

Nobody wants to do a bad job—unless they're saboteurs or self-saboteurs. But as we all know, bad jobs do happen. Sometimes the person's heart really isn't in the job, perhaps because the job is only seen as a paycheck. Sometimes it's the result of lack of preparation, or lack of time to do the job justice. Sometimes it's simple laziness. Perhaps a person is hampered by lack of focus: they can't say no to another assignment, or a scattered and speedy mind keeps them multitasking from one activity to another, avoiding more significant tasks until they're in crisis mode. Whatever the situation, it results in an excellence gap.

None of these situations is inevitable so the question becomes, How do we encourage excellence, in others and in ourselves? A corollary question is, What gets in the way of excellence? Cultivating self-awareness can help illuminate the factors that move you toward excellence, as well as those that derail you. You may be driven by ambition, or pride, or a desire for financial stability; you can inquire into your motivation using the meditation and contemplation techniques recommended. Once you've identified a motive, you can look into its source. Why do you feel that way? Where does that motivation come from and how did you learn to value that?

If ambition motivates you, then ambition for what? Is it power, influence, wealth, or the greater good? Or on the inner, personal side of the ledger, it could be guilt or the lack of self-esteem. If pride motivates you, then pride in what? Pride about your reputation with others, pride in yourself, pride in the company's stock price? If financial stability is the factor, do you have free-floating anxiety about money, or is there a genuine vulnerability to be faced squarely? Again if you seek out the nature and source of the motivation, you can assess its validity for you. Is it right for you, or is it moving you in directions you might—looking from the outside in—rather avoid?

If self-awareness reveals a lack of motivation toward excellence, look into that. Perhaps a fear of making mistakes causes you to hesitate rather than become more engaged. You may sabotage opportunities for job advancement because you fear the challenges of higher position. You may avoid expanding your business for reasons ranging from laziness to risk aversion. You may have adopted successful strategies for simply muddling through, and maybe for some that's okay, but it is unlikely to get you a better job or attract an investor; some investors are even hesitant to go with someone who has never gone broke, thinking that he or she must not have been trying hard enough.

Another attitude that restrains people is fear that success will make them vulnerable. It's no secret that, in addition to admirers, successful people attract competitors who see besting them as a way to advancement. The desire not to be a target can be a powerful motivator: fear of loss may be a stronger catalyst than the possibility of success. If this applies to you, once again, see it first simply as something to note. It may be something you hadn't been aware of and would like to overcome; or self-examination may deliver valuable information about how you want to spend your life. Mindfulness won't tell you the answer but can open up the field for informed decision-making.

In addition to encouraging excellence in ourselves, we often have opportunity to encourage it in others. Sometimes this is in the workplace, especially if you are in a position of helping others to develop. It can also be within your family, attempting to bring your children up with values you treasure, or nurture the aspirations of your spouse. In every case, you can make it your objective to bring out the best in others.

Consider the dreaded performance review. Recently the coaching approach has been gaining currency as a healthier process than merely passing judgment. But whatever the form of an assessment, the challenge is to describe the person's work accurately and to communicate suggestions and/or direction in a way that neither creates resistance to hearing them nor encourages dependency on the person delivering the message.

Few people enjoy being the bearer of bad tidings, so a classic failing in offering feedback arises from softening messages that are hard to hear—those that are negative in their content. But such softening, or even avoidance of the message altogether, sabotages the development of the person addressed, who may have no idea about the shortfalls of his or her performance. Cultivating the ability to work with fear may not make such an encounter more pleasant, but it can allow you to clearly offer constructive insights. It also undercuts the avoidance strategies that might keep you from noticing shortcomings in a person's performance in the first place; after all you may prefer not to recognize the flaws because, if you do, you'll have to address them.

Conversely, failing to see, or at least acknowledge, excellent skills in others may also stem from a fear reaction; having reached a certain professional level, one may avoid recognizing the strengths of others for fear of being displaced by an up-and-comer, extending even so far as subtly sabotaging such a person to undercut the competition. Not only do you owe it to others to be aware of such motivations, you owe it to yourself—to avoid being perceived as a vindictive and cynical person; also, defensiveness and aggression are highly unattractive mental states, capable of poisoning relationships with others and creating a constant state of bad feeling about ourselves.

Encouraging excellence sometimes means training others to be excellent in their work, which may entail demonstrating the attention to detail required for a first-rate job. Sometimes this calls for making many seemingly picky corrections. The work environment is enhanced when this process of thorough supervision is combined with friendly engagement.

After hearing of my protracted illness, one of my former younger colleagues emailed my wife to express his appreciation for the legal training he had received from me, fondly recollecting my "never ending handwritten inserts and innumerable post-it notes." He said he was going home that evening and would drink a martini in my honor, adding that I had introduced him to martinis in the club upstairs from our office, where we sometimes repaired after a full day of work. It's a tribute I cherish, not least because of the balance it expresses. I tried to be thorough without being caught in the perfectionist trap, which is another way of separating yourself from simple presence. Applying mindfulness helped me both to be fully engaged and attentive to detail without compulsiveness and also be able to enjoy and encourage the camaraderie that can make work a pleasure.

Ultimately, encouraging excellence is supported most strongly by getting in the habit of excellence yourself. Whatever you do, whether in work, personal relationships, or family situations, bring an attitude of excellence to it. Examine whether you present yourself in a dignified, uncontrived, and grounded way, as reflected in your bearing, your speech, your attire, and even in the appearance of your office, home, and other surroundings. It is possible to be light-hearted without being frivolous, even when dealing with matters having serious consequences. It is possible to be cheerfully and fully engaged in every moment, and that unforced engagement becomes the basis of a rewarding life, in every situation you encounter.

PART FOUR

4

The Dividends
of Mindfulness

Mindfulness is not just an intermittent activity, it is a powerful way of life. Starting with the general approach of presence and the fear practice, this book has examined the value of mindfulness in situations encountered daily by people in business, law, and other professional pursuits. Mindfulness pays valuable dividends, which become available when you're released from the grip of habitual patterns. They can be brought to bear in every situation, including family life and other activities, regardless of your field of endeavor.

This final section describes some of the strengths that arise from mindfulness disciplines, the "mindfulness muscles" that have been mentioned throughout the book.

Balance

The ability to rest in the present, like ballast in the bottom of a boat, can help keep you steady and on course. By cultivating presence, your relationships and activities have a ground of stability, allowing you to engage with others more fully because you're less distracted. Whether planning, resolving conflicts, or participating in other interpersonal activities, the ability to remain engaged not only facilitates resolution but also communicates to your colleagues that you hear and respect their perspectives.

Familiarity riding emotional responses, including strong reactions, brings confidence that you can handle whatever situation arises without being overwhelmed or alienating others with knee-jerk reactions. Relating mindfully with fear and nervousness—mindful courage—can strengthen your innate connection with presence and enhance your composure and relaxation, even in stressful and challenging situations. Not only is that rewarding personally; it also presents a reassuring presence to those looking to you for leadership or support.

Clarity

Habitual patterns force us into a kind of involuntary multitasking, during which we oscillate between presence and distraction. By reducing the interference of habitual distractions, you see more clearly because you are more present, both on an inner and outer level. On the inner level, enhanced self-awareness allows you to govern your reactions so they do not cloud your perceptions; your practice trains you not to be ensnared by reactivity but to see it as further information to take into account rather than as a mandate you're compelled to enact.

On the outer level you see and hear other people more clearly and notice, for example, whether their speech is congruent with their demeanor. More broadly, you may see the situation not simply from your own point of view but also gain access to the bigger picture: the perspective of the organization itself, its internal politics and other dynamics, and the external environment in which it operates.

Confidence

Once you recognize presence as a reliable basis for engaging in life activities, confidence in its accessibility allows you to be more fluid and skillful in relating with others. No longer needing to rely on your habitual perspectives and strategies, you can open into a broader range of possibilities, further enhancing your effectiveness.

Top-down leadership models are trending out. The notion that one person necessarily has all the answers is a thing of the past. Now the role of an effective leader is to harvest the knowledge, intelligence, and wisdom residing in the people of the organization. Although the leader may be responsible for making the ultimate decision, he or she must communicate effectively to draw out as much useful information as possible. This is an expression of the wisdom of not knowing and genuine humility.

It's also the leader's job to communicate an understanding of the value others bring to the discussion and to encourage expression of perspectives, even those with which he or she may not agree. Genuine humility grounded in confidence is a powerful stance, whatever the role of the person in the organization.

Adaptability

Since change is a reality of life—even when situations seem superficially similar—intelligent and creative responses require flexibility. When you come unstuck from your habitual patterns and responses and develop further confidence, flexibility becomes part of your ordinary way of being.

A variant involves resilience, the ability to recover quickly from difficult conditions. No matter how good a leader, plan, or strategy is, sometimes the world doesn't cooperate; things go wrong, and estimations of future prospects don't pan out. Habitual patterns tend to lock in particular responses, hampering the leader's adaptability to deal with emergencies. The ability to respond with resilience reassures those looking for direction. Resilience also gives the leader the advantage of being able to appraise the situation with clarity and accuracy. Realizing the reality of uncertainty, wise and resilient leaders respond to changing circumstances without panic.

Goodwill

Training in mindfulness enhances a sense of goodwill toward all involved, creating an environment of mutual understanding and respect, and facilitating commitment to organizational and personal goals. This includes not only an organization's executives, staff, and investors but also its customers and suppliers. In addition to fostering a healthy atmosphere throughout the organization, goodwill also applies to individual interactions. A practical benefit of goodwill is that it is easier to deal with people for whom you feel goodwill than those toward whom you feel aversion.

It's easy to feel goodwill toward those who are pleasant and agreeable; it's more of a challenge with those who are difficult or obtuse. The person trained in mindfulness, aware of the power of habitual patterns, recognizes that the difficult ones too struggle with habitual patterns, perhaps even more than the easy-going ones. Knowing the difficulties from personal, internal experience, the mindful person cuts others some slack even while giving them feedback. We are all in the same boat.

APPENDICES

_____

APPENDIX 1: MEDITATION PRACTICE

∞

APPENDIX 2: THE FEAR PRACTICE

∞

APPENDIX 3: CONTEMPLATION

∞

APPENDIX 4: EXERCISES

∞

APPENDIX 5: RECOMMENDED READING

APPENDIX 1: MEDITATION PRACTICE

As presented in this book, the intention of meditation is to cultivate your innate sense of presence by helping you become less distracted. Part One of this book describes what you can expect as a result of the practice.

There are three main steps (and one optional one) in this mindfulness meditation practice:

- ✧ *taking a comfortable, alert posture*
- ✧ *noticing the experience of being present as a human being*
- ✧ *returning to the experience of presence after you notice that you've been caught up in your thoughts*
- ✧ *An optional fourth part is to label thoughts "thinking"*

As you sit in meditation, inevitably you'll notice that you've been caught up in thinking. When that happens, simply come back to the experience of being present with sense perceptions, bodily sensations, and breathing—until you notice again that you've been distracted by your thinking.

Don't be discouraged by the thought-filled quality of meditation or make the mistake of believing that the purpose is to rid ourselves of thoughts. We're just getting familiar with how our minds work, so relax simply with what is. Lots of people do it, and you can, too.

It is the simplicity of the practice that makes it so powerful: you don't distract yourself with theorizing or trying to gauge your progress; just notice the experience of presence in a very basic way, becoming familiar with this ground from which you can be present in every part of your life.

APPENDIX 2: THE FEAR PRACTICE

Before working with the fear practice, spend some time doing meditation practice; it will give you experience in recognizing story lines as different phenomena from simple presence. Simple presence includes not only our sense perceptions but also the emotional content we experience, which includes the fear feeling.

Once you have identified the fear feeling, notice how it shows itself in ordinary life—situations such as the surprise of a ringing phone, or someone accidentally startling you by walking up behind you unnoticed, or meeting with a new customer or client. Let that feeling become familiar so that you just notice it and no longer feel it's a big deal that you have to keep a lid on.

With that experience as background, here are the three steps to working with fear:

✧ *noticing the feeling of fear or nervousness*
✧ *just staying with it, letting it happen, without getting caught up in the story about it our thoughts tell (there's no need to perpetuate the fear feeling—just let it last as long as it does)*
✧ *going ahead with whatever activity you're doing, and starting to notice how connecting with the fear feeling energizes you while you're engaged in the activity*

Especially in the early stages of working with nervousness and fear in this way, you may want to examine the experience using the contemplation practice (see Appendix 3).

APPENDIX 3: CONTEMPLATION

This contemplation technique was first described in the discussion of mindful decision-making in Part Three, and you may want to re-read that to provide additional context. As with the fear practice, the essential introductory practice is to sit in mindfulness meditation practice so that you can discriminate simple presence from being caught up in thinking or a mindset coloring your perceptions.

The state of presence is the ground for contemplation, the starting point. The content of the contemplation is whatever question, issue, or challenge you want to address to uncover fresh insights. Some intentional effort is required to avoid trying to "figure out" the answer or solution, rather than simply resting in presence and allowing insights to arise. Just stay present and let the topic "float," knowing it's there but not trying to work it out. It's probably helpful to set a timer to remind you when the time period you've committed to has elapsed.

In summary, here are the steps of contemplation:

❖ *resting in presence, as if you were meditating*
❖ *knowing the question and letting it "float"*
❖ *not trying to figure out the answer or solution*
   just waiting

If an insight should arise, simply take note of it and use it as further information as you consider the problem or question; remember, an insight can be valuable but needs to be examined to make sure it's actually workable in the situation you're addressing.

APPENDIX 4: EXERCISES

The exercises in this part of the book are designed to help you gain familiarity with the experience of presence and to make it more available—cultivating your mindfulness muscles. You can do these at any time, and once you've become familiar with the meditation experience, your perceptions will be clearer.

Some of them—perhaps all of them—will also provide an opportunity for you to experience the fear feeling. When you complete an exercise, just let go of it. Remember that you don't have to keep track of everything you have done for it to inform your activity and state of mind as you go forward. So do an exercise, and then forget about it, just let it go.

Exercise 1: *Listening to Yourself*

In this exercise recite something that you know by heart. It can be the "Pledge of Allegiance," the Lord's Prayer," a favorite poem, your family's traditional grace before meals, or a passage from your own particular religious background. Just make sure that it's something familiar because the point of this exercise is to bring your attention to your own speaking and not to have to struggle with memory of the particular passage. Here's the exercise:

Do this privately. Start with a few minutes of mindfulness meditation to come back into connection with presence, and then recite the passage in your normal speaking voice and at an ordinary pace—no need to get dramatic, just speak ordinarily. Listen to the sound of your voice, and if you find yourself thinking, whether it's about how you sound or what you're going to have for lunch, simply come back to listening to yourself.

Pause for a few moments, resting in the experience of presence. Repeat the exercise as many times as you like. Then just let it go. If you do this, for example, near the end of a meditation session, leave yourself a few minutes at the end to meditate simply.

Takeaway: This exercise will help you recognize that distraction is a very ordinary experience and that it's possible to stay present while you're speaking.

∞

Exercise 2: *The Telephone Practice*

This is a practice to do at work and is especially useful if you use the phone frequently. It's simply this: when the phone rings (or when you're about to pick up the phone to make a call), put your hand on it and pause for a moment (one ring's worth will do) and notice the experience of presence. Then pick up the phone and proceed. If you use a cell phone, you may want to place it face down so that you don't immediately see who is calling and start thinking about what you'll say.

Takeaway: This exercise will help you recognize that presence is available in completely routine situations, without the need for extensive preparation.

∞

Exercise 3: *Focusing and Opening*

Find a clean and clear space where you can do this exercise and bring along an object to use in the exercise. It can be a flower, a fruit, a stone, a dish, or whatever you have handy. After doing a few minutes of mindfulness meditation to connect with presence, pay attention to the object for a few moments. Then broaden your gaze so that you connect with whatever is in your field of vision. During any part of this, if you find yourself distracted by thoughts, simply come back to focusing on your chosen object, and after a few moments, again open your gaze into your field of vision.

Pause for a few moments, resting in the experience of presence. Repeat the exercise several times if you have time.

Takeaway: This exercise will familiarize you with the difference between focusing your gaze and opening it as if it's the aperture of a wide-angle camera. Unlike Exercise 1, this exercise is silent, so as you become more familiar with it, you can do it in any situation. It's probably easiest with the visual sense, which is so vivid; however, you can also do it with hearing or other sensory perceptions.

Exercise 4: *360° Awareness*

After doing a few minutes of mindfulness meditation to connect with presence, stand in place with an open focus of your gaze, relaxing into your field of vision. Slowly rotate in place allowing whatever comes into your field of vision to be registered in your awareness, like a camera scanning the horizon. If you find yourself focusing on any particular item that comes into view, just relax into your broad field of vision. During any part of this, if you find yourself distracted by thoughts, simply come back to the exercise. When you reach your starting point, stand there with your vision open.

Takeaway: Like Exercise 2, this exercise will familiarize you with the experience of unfixated vision and the ability to distinguish it from staring at a particular spot or object, which is another form of distraction (if it's not done intentionally). The difference is that you'll be doing this while you're in motion. You will notice that this is available in any situation, not just one of formal practice.

Exercise 5: *Taking a Walk*

After doing a few minutes of mindfulness meditation, find a pleasant place to take a walk for 10 or 15 minutes, or longer if you like. Decide in advance how long you'll walk, and then just walk, avoiding any particular agenda, whether it's finding mushrooms, identifying plants and trees, recognizing geological formations, or whatever. Just walk with your vision, hearing, and other senses open, taking in whatever you encounter. If you find yourself distracted by thoughts, simply let go of them and come back to walking with open awareness. If you encounter other people, relate to them as you ordinarily would (the idea is not to seem like a weirdo), and when they're gone, come back to this walking exercise. When your walking time is over, return to your starting point where you did the initial mindfulness meditation. Notice whether anything changes about your state of mind and awareness of presence after you consider the exercise to be completed.

Takeaway: This exercise is intended to broaden your scope of applying mindfulness so that presence is available in a variety of situations.

Exercise 6: *Speaking to (and Listening to) another Person*

This exercise is done with a partner, someone who is willing to do a mindfulness exercise with you. A person who is already involved with mindfulness discipline will be helpful. As with Exercise 1, find a quiet and private place for the exercise and begin with a few minutes of meditation to firm up the connection with presence. Decide who will go first and decide on a time; if possible, set a timer so nobody has to keep glancing at a watch. The first to speak has two tasks:

the first is to listen to his or her own voice (see Exercise 1); the second is to be aware of any emotional tone (including fear or nervousness) experienced while speaking, including during any gaps in the speaking. The listener (who only listens and doesn't talk) has three tasks: one is to listen to the other person's voice; another is to be aware of any distractedness from listening; and the third is to be aware of any emotional tone (including fear or nervousness) experienced while listening to the other person.

Takeaway: This exercise ups the mindfulness ante by working to cultivate mindfulness while relating to another person. Issues of distractedness and emotional tone are clarified by this exercise.

∞

Exercise 7: *Listening to Music*

This exercise can be done alone or with other people. As usual, start with a few minutes of meditation to clarify the connection with presence. In this exercise, listen to a variety of kinds of music and notice the emotional tone evoked by each and how they're different. My preference is for instrumental music since there is less likelihood of getting caught up in the words, but you may have a different preference. The important factor here is to use a variety of different kinds of music, and a digital device may allow you to pre-select a number of album cuts so that you don't have to interrupt the listening experience by changing CDs or vinyl records; if that's not available, just remember to continue in presence as you make those changes.

Takeaway: This exercise focuses on recognizing emotional responses to nonverbal stimuli, recognizing how your response to a particular artist or composer or type of music differs from your response to others. Don't over-analyze; just enjoy the experience; you may notice things you hadn't noticed before. You may also notice changes in your musical taste, finding that you actually enjoy opera or hip-hop when previously you thought that you couldn't abide it!

Exercise 8: *Driving Your Car (or Riding Public Transportation)*

Because you can connect with presence in any situation, finding a regular time for that (aside from formal sitting practice) can be helpful. Because most of us travel to work daily, using that time can be helpful in establishing the universal availability of presence. If you're driving to work, just turn off the radio or stereo and notice how you can be present in the car as it moves down the road. With presence, you'll notice the landscape around you (whether constructed or natural), details about your vehicle, and whatever else comes to your attention. Make it a relaxed experience without trying to hold tightly to any of those experiences; just let them happen naturally. If you're taking public transportation (whether bus, train, or airplane), turn off your electronic equipment and notice your surroundings, both within the vehicle—other passengers—and outside.

Takeaway: This exercise will help you see that you can connect with presence anywhere, anytime.

APPENDIX 5: RECOMMENDED READING

Carroll, Michael. *Awake at Work*. Boston: Shambhala, 2004.

—. *The Mindful Leader*. Boston: Shambhala, 2007.

—. *Fearless at Work*. Boston: Shambhala, 2012.

de Becker, Gavin. *The Gift of Fear*. New York: Dell, 1999.

Goleman, Daniel, Richard Boyatzis, and Annie McKee. *Primal Leadership: Realizing the Power of Emotional Intelligence*. Boston: Harvard Business Review Press, 2002.

Kahneman, Daniel. *Thinking, Fast and Slow*. New York: Farrar, Strauss & Giroux, 2011.

Kofman, Fred. *Conscious Business: How to Build Value through Values*. Louisville, CO: Sounds True, 2006.

Lesser, Marc. *LESS: Accomplishing More by Doing Less*. Novato, CA: New World Library, 2009.

Marturano, Janice. *Finding the Space to Lead: A Practical Guide to Mindful Leadership*. New York: Bloomsbury Press, 2014.

Riskin, Leonard L. *The Contemplative Lawyer: On the Potential Contributions of Mindfulness Meditation to Law Students, Lawyers, and their Clients*, Harvard Negotiation Law Review 1, Spring 2002.

Rogers, Scott L., M.S., J.D. *The Six Minute Solution: A Mindfulness Primer for Lawyers*, Mindful Living Press 2009.

Walker, Sidney C., *Trust Your Gut: How to Overcome the Obstacles to Greater Success and Self-Fulfillment*. Long Beach: High Plains Publications, 2004.

About the Author

P ATTON HYMAN, ESQ., is President and Executive Director of Applied Mindfulness Training, Inc., a nonprofit corporation that presents retreats and programs geared toward applying contemplative disciplines in the professions, business, and the arts. He has taught meditation, including teacher trainings, for over 30 years. Patton practiced for decades in a large Atlanta firm and was a solo practitioner in Barnet, Vermont, specializing in estate planning and property and business transactions. For more: *www.appliedminfulnesstraining.org*

Made in the USA
Columbia, SC
01 July 2020